the chinese
takeout cookbook

the
chinese takeout
cookbook

quick and easy dishes to prepare at home

diana kuan

ballantine books / new york

Published in the United States by Ballantine Books,
an imprint of The Random House Publishing Group,
a division of Random House, Inc., New York.

BALLANTINE and colophon are registered
trademarks of Random House, Inc.

All photographs by the author except for those on pages 28, 30, 36,
and 38 which are by Ethan Finkelstein, and page 40 which are by
Christopher Rogala and reprinted here by permission of the photographers.

ISBN 978-0-345-52912-1

eISBN 978-0-345-52914-5

Printed in China on acid-free paper

www.ballantinebooks.com

2 4 6 8 9 7 5 3 1

FIRST EDITION

Book design by Barbara M. Bachman

In memory of my dad,
Tony Kwong Shing Kuan,
who was always happiest at the dinner table,
surrounded by good food and good company

contents

introduction

chinese in america

Sit back for a moment and imagine biting into a warm, savory egg roll. Or a juicy pork dumpling. Or for that matter, a spicy morsel of General Tso's Chicken (page 70). Although the flavors vary from food to food, chances are we're all imagining the same feeling: satisfaction.

Chinese takeout is in many ways an all-American cuisine. Many of us grew up eating as much Chinese food as we did hamburgers and hot dogs. It's comfort food that has played a supporting role on many occasions, from potlucks to poker nights, from late-night study sessions to cross-country road trips. Whether you're in Brooklyn, Bozeman, or Biloxi, Chinese restaurants are ubiquitous. If you live in an urban area, chances are your kitchen drawers are filled to the brim with takeout menus, soy sauce packets, and disposable chopsticks.

American-style Chinese food predates the arrival of most regional Chinese cuisines that we now enjoy, including Sichuan, Hunan, and Fujianese. The first Chinese restaurants in the United States were opened in California in the late 1840s and 1850s, during the gold rush, by Cantonese immigrants who, due to prejudice, had a hard time finding work on the railroads. Most cooks taught themselves, re-creating foods from home with the ingredients they found in this strange new world. Restaurants in the mining towns catered to both Chinese and non-Chinese laborers; the food was cheap and came in hefty portions. In San Francisco more upscale restaurants drew urban sophisticates who were curious about the "exotic" dishes and eager to report back to their friends. When the Chinese and non-Chinese railroad workers began migrating east, the restaurants followed and flourished, especially in cities.

By the early twentieth century, popular Chinese dishes had become part of the cultural vernacular. Artist Edward Hopper produced a painting in 1929 that he titled *Chop Suey,* in which two women idle in a Chinese eatery over a pot of tea. In his novel *Main Street,* Sinclair Lewis describes how his city girl main character tries to introduce chow mein and other Chinese foods to her suburban neighbors in 1920s Minnesota. And the poet Carl Sandburg mentions egg foo young in his 1936 epic poem "The People, Yes." (More recently, episodes of popular shows from *Seinfeld* to *Sex and the City* have depicted Chinese restaurants and Chinese takeout as being ingrained in the lives of their characters.)

At midcentury, Chinese restaurants had become fashionable hangouts for young urbanites. At the Cotton Club in New York, you could order chow mein or fried rice along with your gin fizz. In California, tiki restaurants, spearheaded by the Trader Vic's chain and Don the Beachcomber, created an entire dining experience around pupu platters of egg rolls, barbecued ribs, and wontons, with mai tais and Singapore slings to wash down all the food. In Manhattan in the 1970s, the concept of Chinese food delivery exploded in popularity. Soon, Chinese restaurants and the idea of takeout spread to the suburbs and small towns and became entrenched in the daily lives of millions of Americans.

Today there are more than forty thousand Chinese restaurants in the United States, and more are opening every day. Some have even made their versions of Chinese dishes into popular local specialties: You can order up kalua pork-steamed buns in Hawaii, chow mein sandwiches in Rhode Island, or soy vinegar crayfish in Louisiana. What began in this country as exotic has become thoroughly American.

American-Chinese food is a natural by-product of Chinese immigration, but it can be just as good as food eaten in mainland China. I avoid using the word "authentic" whenever possible, because all cuisines have evolved from somewhere, whether it be Cajun food, Italian food (tomato sauce was nonexistent in Italy until the late 1600s), American-Chinese food, or even Chinese food in China. Food almost always changes, and needs to change, across provinces, countries, and continents, adapting along the way to use local ingredients and to suit local tastes. If a chef needs to alter a dish, it's not a travesty as long as he or she does it well and with care. Without cross-cultural fusion of cuisines, we wouldn't have bagels with lox, deep-dish pizza, hamburgers, baked ziti, jambalaya, and many other

iconic foods in America. Likewise, American-Chinese classics, such as chow mein and Shrimp with Lobster Sauce (page 110), are also products of the American story, and delicious if cooked with care.

My own American story involved Chinese food that came in many different forms. When I was five, my family emigrated from China to Puerto Rico, where my parents worked at a Chinese-Latin restaurant that served entrées such as lo mein with a side of plantains. Later, when we moved to suburban Massachusetts, they helped my extended family run a Polynesian-style eatery where customers chowed down on Crab Rangoon (page 34), fried egg rolls, and Pineapple Fried Rice (page 151). The food my family served at work wasn't much like the Cantonese food they cooked at home, but what they served were the product of the American melting pot, authentic in their own right. Most important, my family knew that customers found their piping-hot plates of stir-fries and noodles comforting and satisfying.

I was living in Beijing in 2007 when I started my blog, Appetite for China. In it, I recorded meals I ate around the city and interesting recipes I found in my travels around the country. I thought of the blog as a way to share with readers the everyday foods, particularly lesser-known regional specialties, eaten around China. What I didn't expect were readers back home in the United States emailing again and again, asking for recipes for dishes they grew up eating at Chinese restaurants in their own hometowns. How do you get the perfect crunchy exterior for General Tso's Chicken (page 70)? How do you fold a wonton? How do you make flavorful Hot and Sour Soup (page 52) without MSG? How do I get the rich red exterior on Chinese Barbecued Pork (page 97) without food coloring?

So here it is: a collection of more than eighty recipes for making your favorite restaurant Chinese foods at home. Additives such as MSG and food coloring have been eliminated, and a few vegetarian variations have been included, but otherwise the dishes are true to their tasty, saucy, nostalgia-inducing origins. Most, like Orange Chicken (page 76) and Moo Shu Pork (page 100), are takeout classics. Others, like Lobster Cantonese (page 112) and Mini Egg Tarts (page 167), have been staples of American Chinatowns for generations. And you don't even need to live near an Asian market or own a deep fryer to make all this mouthwatering food: Most of the ingredients can be found in your local supermarkets, and a wok or heavy-bottom pot, along with a fine-mesh strainer, work well for all the frying recipes in this book. So put those takeout menus back in the drawers, roll up your sleeves, and let's get cooking!

the chinese
takeout cookbook

the chinese pantry

ingredients

Ingredients used in Chinese cooking can be found in Asian markets, the international aisles of supermarkets, and increasingly online (see Resources, page 179). Below is a list of common items used in the recipes in this book.

vegetables

BAMBOO SHOOTS The tender and edible stems of the bamboo plant are called bamboo shoots. While fresh bamboo shoots are hard to find, canned bamboo shoots are available year-round in most supermarkets. You can buy them as slices or thin strips. Once the cans are open, the shoots can be stored in a water-filled container in the fridge for up to two weeks; just be sure to change the water every other day.

BEAN SPROUTS Short for "mung bean sprouts," bean sprouts are about three inches long with small yellow heads and are sold fresh at both Chinese and Western markets. They shouldn't be confused with soybean sprouts, which are greenish and more curled. When buying mung bean sprouts, select the sprouts with crisp white bodies, without any browning. The Chinese usually pluck off the head (bean) and tail (root) of the sprouts for aesthetic and textural purposes, though both the head and tail are still perfectly edible. Use the sprouts on the day of purchase or store them in your fridge's produce crisper bin in a plastic bag for up to three days.

BOK CHOY This member of the cabbage family is a versatile vegetable that can be used in a number of ways, from stir-frying to steaming to soups. Regular bok choy, which are almost a foot long, are also called *bok choy sum,* or "heart" of the bok choy. The recipes in this book, however, call for either regular small baby bok choy, about 3 inches long, with bright white stems and dark green leaves, or the slightly larger variety of baby bok choy called Shanghai bok choy, about 4 inches long, which have pale yellow stems and lighter green leaves. When shopping, look for crisp stalks and leaves that aren't wilting.

CHILI PEPPERS In Chinese cuisine, fresh bird's-eye chilies, also called Thai chilies, are often chopped and made into chili sauce. Dried chilies, on the other hand, are stir-fried into dishes such as Kung Pao Chicken (page 65) and Dry-Fried Green Beans (page 128) to add a smoky, spicy flavor. You can keep them whole or, for a much spicier dish, split the chilies in half lengthwise to release the seeds, which contain most of the heat.

CHINESE BROCCOLI Called *gai lan* in Cantonese, Chinese broccoli is sold in large bunches year-round in Chinese markets. Instead of the big florets that Western broccoli has, Chinese broccoli has thick glossy leaves. It's also slightly more bitter in its raw state than its Western counterpart. Select the bunch with dark green, crisp leaves and small closed white buds that are somewhat hidden within the leaves. Yellowing leaves and open flowers indicate the broccoli isn't very fresh.

CHINESE EGGPLANT Unlike Western eggplant, Chinese eggplant is long and slender in appearance and less bitter in taste. Look for eggplants with smooth exteriors, a firm texture, and little to no bruising in the lavender skin.

CILANTRO Also known as fresh coriander, cilantro is frequently used in Chinese cuisine to both heighten other flavors and cut the richness of a dish, for example, for Taiwanese-Style Pork Belly Buns (page 46). It is also used extensively to cook with and to garnish seafood.

GINGER One of the key ingredients in almost all Chinese dishes, ginger is part of the flavor trifecta of Chinese seasonings, along with garlic and scallions. In stir-frying, the three are often cooked first before the other ingredients, forming a strong flavor base. Ginger's clean sharpness makes both seafood and meat taste fresher, and also cuts the richness of fatty dishes. Look for ginger that is heavy and hard; lightness in weight and wrinkled skin indicate that it's not very fresh. Ginger should always be peeled before use (see The Flavor Trifecta: Ginger, Garlic, and Scallions, page 10–11).

NAPA CABBAGE This Asian cabbage variety is more oblong than green cabbage, with white or yellow crinkly leaves. Napa cabbage is commonly used in stir-frying and braising, or as a dumpling filling because of its delicate flavor. It can be stored in the crisper bin of the refrigerator for up to a week.

SCALLIONS Also called green onions, it adds a delicious onion flavor to dishes ranging from stir-fries to dumplings to Scallion Pancakes (page 37). Often, a recipe will specify white parts only, green parts only, or both white and green parts. The general rule is that white parts, which have a stronger flavor, are used at the beginning of cooking, whereas the milder green parts are used toward the end of cooking or as a garnish. The traditional way to slice scallions is at an angle to expose more of the flavorful insides. See The Flavor Trifecta: Ginger, Garlic, and Scallions on page 10–11.

SHIITAKE MUSHROOMS The most commonly used mushrooms in Chinese cooking are sold both fresh and dried. Fresh shiitakes are widely available in Western markets. When preparing fresh shiitake mushrooms, be sure to wipe the caps clean with a damp towel and remove the stems. Dried shiitakes are most easily found in Asian markets. They have an earthy aroma and contribute an umami flavor that is prized in Chinese cooking. The best dried shiitakes have thick caps with white fissures on top. Both types of shiitakes are extremely versatile; they can be stir-fried, steamed, grilled, braised, or added to soups.

TOFU Sometimes called bean curd, tofu is formed by pressing soy milk solids into blocks. It's sold in a few different varieties. The best types of tofu to use for stir-frying and braising are firm or extra firm. Soft tofu is good for simmering in soups or adding at the end in cooking Mapo Tofu (page 123). Once a sealed package of tofu is opened, use the tofu within three days.

WATER CHESTNUTS Lightly sweet in flavor, water chestnuts add a refreshing crispness to many Chinese dishes. Few Asian markets have them fresh, so it's easiest to buy them canned in supermarkets. Just drain and discard the canning liquid and chop or slice the water chestnuts before use.

clockwise from top left:
Shanghai bok choy,
baby bok choy,
Chinese broccoli,
Chinese water spinach

WATER SPINACH With stalks about 1½ feet long and narrow pointed leaves, water spinach is sold in Asian markets in very large bunches. The stalks are most commonly stir-fried, with a minimal amount of seasonings. (If water spinach is unavailable, you can substitute watercress or regular spinach.) While the bunch will look enormous, it actually cooks down a lot in the wok. To use, trim the thicker bottom half of the stems, then cut the remaining top half of the stems and the leaves into 3-inch lengths.

sauces, wines, vinegars, and other condiments

BEAN SAUCE This staple of Sichuan and Hunan cooking, also known as yellow bean paste, is made from fermented soybeans. An opened jar with a tight-fitting lid will keep indefinitely in the back of the fridge.

CHILI BEAN SAUCE This spicy bean sauce is simply bean sauce spiked with chili oil or chili paste. Some brands include other flavorings, such as garlic, sesame oil, sugar, rice wine, and salt. As a substitute you can mix equal parts bean sauce and chili sauce.

CHILI SAUCE AND CHILI GARLIC SAUCE Chinese chili sauces make a wonderful spicy addition to stir-fries. In recipes that call for chili sauce, you can also substitute chili garlic sauces that don't have a very pronounced garlic flavor, such as the chili garlic sauce from Huy Fong Foods. Louisiana hot sauce is also a great substitute for Asian chili sauces. If you would like to try making your own chili sauce, see Basic Chili Sauce (page 174).

CHILI OIL This bright reddish-orange oil is made by flavoring vegetable oil with dried red chili flakes. You can buy it in most supermarkets, or make your own (see Homemade Chili Oil, page 175).

CHINESE RICE WINE Recipes that call for Chinese rice wine often list the ingredient as yellow rice wine or Shaoxing rice wine. Shaoxing is the name of China's most well-known rice wine, a bargain at $3 or $4 a bottle and widely available in Asian markets. Look for the red-labeled Pagoda brand bottles; the yellow-labeled bottles are sweetened. Avoid other kinds of "Shaoxing cooking wine" from mainland China; they're poor-quality imitators and often salted. If you can't find Pagoda brand Shaoxing, dry sherry is a great substitute. Mirin, a Japanese rice wine, is not a recommended substitute in Chinese cooking because of its sweetness.

COOKING OILS The best types of oil to use for stir-frying or deep-frying are peanut oil, vegetable oil, and canola oil because of their high smoke points. Olive oil, which has a low smoke point, is okay for cooking at medium temperatures, but it should never be used for deep-frying or stir-frying at high temperatures.

FISH SAUCE Although fish sauce is best known for being a Southeast Asian condiment, it is actually used a fair amount in Cantonese cooking. It's made by fermenting fish, usually anchovies, and is extremely pungent. Use sparingly; even a few drops will provide plenty of flavor. Well-refrigerated bottles will keep for at least a year.

HOISIN SAUCE This versatile sweetened soybean paste is mixed with flavorings such as garlic and vinegar. You can use it as a marinade for roast pork and spareribs, as a sauce ingredient for Moo Shu Pork (page 100) and other stir-fries, or as a dip for roast duck.

OYSTER SAUCE A staple of Cantonese cooking, oyster sauce has been used in the United States since the early days of chow mein and Chop Suey (page 147). This dark, viscous sauce is made from oysters (or oyster extract), water, and salt. (Vegetarian oyster sauces are flavored with mushrooms.) Most brands nowadays also have cornstarch and caramel coloring. A recommended brand is Lee Kum Kee, which has been producing oyster sauce since the late 1800s.

PLUM SAUCE This popular sweet-and-sour condiment is made from plums, vinegar, sugar, and a tiny bit of chili. It's a great dip for appetizers such as spareribs, egg rolls, and fried wontons. It's also a popular condiment for roast duck. Duck sauce is a version of plum sauce created with other fruits, such as apples and apricots, though it often contains a high percentage of additives.

SESAME OIL Whether used as a sauce ingredient or drizzled on after cooking, sesame oil adds a lovely nutty aroma to Chinese dishes. For the recipes in this book, use Chinese or Japanese sesame oil, which is toasted and dark in color, instead of Middle Eastern light-colored sesame oil from raw sesame seeds. Buy sesame oil that is sold in glass bottles, because plastic makes oil become rancid more quickly.

SOY SAUCE AND DARK SOY SAUCE Both types of soy sauce are dark, salty, and earthy, used for seasoning food while cooking or at the table. Most of the recipes in this book call for regular soy

the flavor trifecta:

ginger, garlic, and scallions

Many recipes in this book will call for ginger, garlic, and scallions. This trifecta of Chinese flavorings forms the base of much of Chinese cooking. Here is how to prepare these aromatic ingredients as called for in the recipes.

from top left:
minced ginger, grated ginger, julienned ginger, sliced ginger

middle row, from left:
minced garlic, crushed garlic

bottom row from left:
chopped scallions, julienned scallions, sliced scallions

sauce. Dark soy sauce, aged longer with molasses added at the end of processing, is thicker, slightly sweeter, and a tad less salty; it adds a great deep flavor and natural deep red coloring to dishes such as Chinese Barbecued Pork (page 97) and Classic Barbecued Spareribs (page 33). Whichever brand you choose, make sure soybeans are one of the main ingredients; many brands use hydrolyzed vegetable protein to imitate a soy flavor. Low-sodium soy sauce is a good substitute if it is made with soybeans and not artificial ingredients.

VINEGARS

- CHINESE BLACK VINEGAR Slightly smoky with a pleasant sweet aroma, this aged dark vinegar is reminiscent of good balsamic vinegar, which can be used as a substitute. The best black vinegar to look for is Gold Plum brand Chinkiang Vinegar, available in almost all Chinese markets.

- CHINESE WHITE RICE VINEGAR This clear rice vinegar adds a sharp, acidic flavor to Chinese dishes. In a pinch, cider vinegar is a decent substitute. Don't use distilled malt vinegar as a substitute, as the flavor is much too sharp.

spices

CRUSHED RED PEPPER FLAKES Packaged red pepper flakes found in supermarkets are dried chilies that have been coarsely pounded with their seeds. They're quite powerful, so taste the dishes first with the amount suggested in the recipes before adding more.

CUMIN Best known for its pervasiveness in Indian and Middle Eastern cooking, cumin is also frequently used in China in dishes that have been influenced by the Islamic Chinese. You can buy cumin preground or as whole seeds. While preground cumin is convenient, buying whole seeds, then toasting and grinding them before use, will make a dish much more fragrant.

FIVE-SPICE POWDER Chinese five-spice powder is a fragrant ground blend of star anise, cinnamon, cloves, Sichuan pepper, and fennel. Depending on the brand, sometimes ground ginger is also added. Chinese five-spice powder is often sold in spice bottles at Western supermarkets. If you buy larger bags at a Chinese market, transfer the contents to an airtight jar. It's best stored in a cool, dry pantry.

SICHUAN PEPPER/SICHUAN PEPPERCORNS All the recipes in this book that call for Sichuan pepper refer to the ground form of Sichuan peppercorns. Sichuan peppercorns may look like the red version of black or white peppercorns, but they are actually tiny berries. They are best known for their numbing spiciness, but they also have wonderful floral characteristics. You can find whole Sichuan peppercorns in Chinese markets; they should be dry-roasted on a skillet, then ground before use. The gourmet brand Frontier Natural Products sells very fresh-tasting Sichuan peppercorns in a grinder; the product is available at Whole Foods and other markets. You can also buy Sichuan peppercorns online at www.penzeys.com (see Resources, page 179). In a pinch, crushed red pepper flakes or cayenne pepper can be substituted, but neither really has the same floral notes and complexity that Sichuan pepper does.

STAR ANISE The Chinese often use whole star anise to flavor cooking liquids for meat and poultry. It has a mild licorice flavor that pairs well with cinnamon, which it is often used alongside. Star anise is also one of the spices in Chinese five-spice powder.

noodles and other dried products

BEAN THREAD NOODLES Also called thin glass noodles, these translucent threadlike noodles are made from mung beans and sold dry. They look a lot like the whiter rice vermicelli noodles, but don't confuse the two. Bean thread noodles are used more often in braises, soups, and salads rather than stir-frying.

CORNSTARCH In Chinese cooking cornstarch has three main roles. It's often added to marinades, not to tenderize, but rather to form a protective seal around the meat and lock in flavor and moisture for stir-frying. Chinese cooks also use cornstarch to coat meat for deep-frying to get a light crunchy exterior. And it works wonders as a sauce thickener, giving body to a thin sauce in just seconds.

DRIED SHRIMP Dried shrimp add a briny earthiness to anything from soup broth to stir-fried vegetables. Choose the kind that are larger and reddish orange, and avoid the tinier white opaque shrimp with visible black eyes, which can be pretty bland.

EGG NOODLES Chinese egg noodles, made with wheat flour and eggs, are great for stir-frying or simply mixing with a cooked sauce. Look for noodles that are pale yellow in color rather than those with a bright yellow hue, which indicates the use of food coloring.

clockwise from top left: chinese fermented black beans, dried shrimp, whole and ground Sichuan pepper, dried red chilies, lily buds, star anise, dried shiitake mushrooms

FERMENTED BLACK BEANS Also called Chinese dried black beans, fermented black beans are usually sold in plastic packages. Transfer the contents to an airtight storage container immediately after opening and store them in the back of the fridge, where they will keep indefinitely. Right before using, just rinse the beans under cold water to rehydrate them and remove excess grit.

LILY BUDS Sometimes called golden needles because of their yellowish color and thin shape, lily buds are often used in vegetarian dishes such as Buddha's Delight (page 126). They should be soaked before use and the strands separated.

RICE VERMICELLI NOODLES Made with rice flour, rice vermicelli noodles are white and about the diameter of angel hair pasta. Sometimes called rice stick noodles, they can be used for stir-fries as well as soups.

SESAME SEEDS (WHITE OR BLACK) These tiny seeds are often used in Chinese cooking to add a nutty, sweet aroma to the finished dish. White sesame seeds are raw and can be used as is, but your dish will taste even better if the seeds are toasted briefly in a dry pan beforehand. Black sesame seeds are preroasted and often used in desserts, such as Black Sesame Ice Cream (page 168).

WHEAT NOODLES Made with wheat flour and water, wheat noodles are traditionally used in northern China and other places where wheat is abundant. They're wonderful in tossed noodle dishes like Dan Dan Noodles (page 137) or noodle soups like Taiwanese Beef Noodle Soup (page 143), but are often too starchy for stir-frying. For stir-frying, see Egg Noodles (page 13).

equipment

In addition to a wok, there are a few key items to invest in for your kitchen that will make your Chinese cooking easier and more enjoyable. In decades past one had to track down a Chinese supermarket or Chinese restaurant supply store to purchase such equipment, but in recent years major kitchenware retailers, such as Crate & Barrel, Sur La Table, and Bed Bath & Beyond (see Resources, page 179, for more places to find supplies for your kitchen), have started carrying items specifically designed for Chinese cooking.

BAMBOO SKIMMER Bamboo skimmers, also called strainers or spiders, have long bamboo handles with wire mesh baskets. They serve dual purposes: You can skim excess thick foam from soups and stocks, or scoop up food when deep-frying or blanching.

BAMBOO STEAMERS These steamers are often sold in three-piece sets, with two trays and one lid. They are fantastic for steaming a variety of Chinese dishes, including fish, dumplings, and vegetables.

JULIENNE PEELER This is an amazing time-saving tool for cutting fine strips of many vegetables and fruits, including cucumbers, carrots, apples, and potatoes. Lay whatever you're julienning flat on a cutting board, holding one end down with your fingers or a fork. Then, starting at least an inch away from where you're holding, use the peeler to slice away from you into strips.

KNIVES Contrary to some beliefs, you don't need a cleaver to cook Chinese food. A well-made 8- or 10-inch chef's knife works well for all the recipes in this book; it is one of the first things you should buy for a well-stocked kitchen. In place of a chef's knife, you can also buy a 7-inch Japanese-style santoku knife, which is lighter in weight and has fluted blades to prevent food from sticking to the blade. Whichever knife you choose, make sure the handle fits comfortably in your hand. Make sure to keep your knives well sharpened. Bring them to a professional knife sharpener every six to twelve months, depending on how much cooking you do.

MEZZALUNA A mezzaluna is not a necessary purchase if you have a great chef's knife, but for cooks who finds themselves constantly mincing garlic and chopping herbs, a mezzaluna is a practical tool to have for relieving some of the wrist tension from constant chopping. The knife has one or two blades with a handle on each end and chops by being rocked back and forth. (*Mezzaluna* means "half-moon" in Italian.) KitchenAid makes a very good basic model for around $17, or you can spend a bit more for double-blade versions or ones that come with their own cutting board with a shallow, rounded bowl-shaped center for holding in chopped bits.

MICROPLANE GRATER A Microplane grater is perfect for grating ginger and extracting ginger juice. The ginger flesh and juice come out of the underside, while the tough fibrous parts remain on top to be discarded. You can substitute the finest grade on a cheese grater.

MORTAR AND PESTLE If you don't own a spice grinder, a mortar with a pestle is great for crushing spices such as Sichuan peppercorns and cumin after you toast them on the stove.

OIL THERMOMETER An instant-read oil thermometer, also called a candy thermometer, is essential for accurate deep-frying. A good thermometer averages around $15, and will let you know precisely when to add your food. This prevents the food from absorbing too much cold oil when it is added too early or quickly burning when added too late.

RICE COOKER These fail-proof cookers free up the stove top and allow you to focus on entrées and sides without worrying about the timing of rice cooking in the pot. Basic models start at around $30, though there are more high-tech rice cookers available now that have precision timing and settings for different types of rice. Some rice cookers also come with food steamer inserts, so you can steam vegetables while you cook your rice.

STEAMER RINGS AND STEAMER INSERTS In place of bamboo steamers, you can also steam food by setting a plate on top of a metal steamer rack or collapsible steamer insert that folds open like a lily pad. They are a bit harder to find than bamboo steamer baskets, but still available at large Chinese markets and other retailers.

TONGS Sturdy, well-made tongs are essential for tossing noodles, transferring food when you're deep-frying, or flipping meats when roasting.

WOK See Wok Basics.

WOK SPATULA While wok cooking can be done with metal and wooden spoons and regular spatulas, the most versatile utensil is a wok spatula. This wide, shovel-shape spatula has rounded edges that match the curves inside the wok, allowing you to scoop up food bits and sauces easily. The best kind of wok spatula to buy is stainless steel, because of its ability to withstand high temperatures and the ease of cleaning it. Silicone spatulas tend to melt around the edges over time from the high heat used in wok cooking.

wok basics

If you are looking forward to doing a fair amount of Chinese cooking, I recommend investing in a wok. For years, I stir-fried regularly in my trusty 12-inch stainless steel skillet, but was often annoyed by the food sticking to the pan or spilling out from all the stirring. It wasn't until I moved to China in 2007 and started cooking regularly with a wok that I realized how useful it was. I could stir-fry a dish for a dinner party without needing to do it in two batches. I could deep-fry egg rolls. I could steam dumplings. I could braise, boil, poach, smoke, or make Chicken Stock (page 172). Even hefty Western dishes such as beef bourguignon and osso buco were easier in a wok. A wok, with its sloping edges, heats up fast and retains heat well, ensuring that everything inside cooks evenly.

A well-made carbon steel or cast-iron wok costs only $20 or $30 and will last you a lifetime. The best and most versatile wok is 14 inches in diameter, which is ideal for cooking for four to six people, depending on the dish. If you're buying a new wok, try to find one that comes with a lid. If you need to buy a lid separately, shop around at a kitchen supply store for one that is slightly smaller than the width of your wok, so that it fits just below the top edge. For example, buy a 13-inch lid for a 14-inch wok.

choosing a wok

CARBON STEEL This lightweight but incredibly strong vessel heats up and cools down quickly, retains heat well, and, once it's seasoned, produces an even sear when stir-frying. It is my wok of choice. It helps generate what Cantonese cooks call "wok hay," literally translated to "breath of a wok," or the liveliness of a dish that results from cooking food at just the right temperature for just the right amount of time. Look for a carbon steel wok with a flat bottom, which allows the wok to sit on the stove without a wok ring, and a long handle, making it easier to maneuver. (When using woks with two short handles, you must use potholders or a kitchen towel to move or even touch the wok, which makes it more awkward, especially if you have a spatula in one hand.) Carbon steel woks need to be seasoned before use (see Seasoning a Wok, page 20), but over time they develop a lovely black patina that's essential to great stir-frying.

CAST IRON Cooks in China have been using cast-iron woks for centuries. The most common cast-iron woks come with two short metal handles and have a rounded bottom. The sloping bottom is a traditional design, from back when people made food by setting their cooking vessels in a ring over an open flame. For use on a conventional gas stove, a rounded-bottom wok needs to be set on a similar metal ring. Rounded-bottom woks cannot be used on an electric stove. Cast-iron woks are excellent for retaining heat, but they take longer to heat up and longer to cool down than carbon steel, which means food needs to be removed quickly after cooking or it can burn. They also tend to be heavier than carbon steel woks. If you're still in the market for cast iron, look for woks with flat bottoms and long handles. Like carbon steel woks, cast-iron woks also need to be seasoned (see Seasoning a Wok, page 20).

STAINLESS STEEL SKILLET Stainless steel skillets are the best alternative to using a wok. They don't have the natural nonstick coating of well-seasoned carbon steel or cast-iron woks, but they are easy to maintain (no seasoning, can be scrubbed with soap, and are dishwasher safe). A 12-inch skillet is a good size to use for stir-frying for one to two people, though a 14-inch skillet is best for four. Because the cooking surface of a skillet is smaller than that of a wok, and because the sides are lower, you will have to be a little more careful with stir-frying to keep food from spilling out. You don't have to shell out for expensive skillets either; a good, sturdy stainless steel skillet from a kitchenware store starts at $30 or $40. There are a few recipes in the book, however, for which a wok is essential; this is noted in the individual recipes.

NONSTICK WOKS AND SKILLETS   Nonstick pans are good for panfrying dumplings and Scallion Pancakes (page 37) and egg dishes like Egg Foo Young with Gravy (page 120), but they are not the best choice for extensive Chinese cooking. Over time, the nonstick coatings are likely to wear off from the high heat used in stir-frying. For cooking most of the recipes in this book, it's best to buy a wok or large stainless steel skillet.

seasoning a wok

Seasoning a wok is a one- to two-hour-long process that will start you down the path to great Chinese cooking. Follow these steps and you'll be using your wok in no time.

1. Scrub the new wok with a scouring sponge or steel wool and hot soapy water to remove any factory coatings. Set the wok on the stove for 1 to 2 minutes over high heat to dry. The wok is completely dry if all the water beads have evaporated.

2. Take 2 to 3 scallions and trim off the hard bottom end and the green parts. Leave the white segments whole. Put the wok over high heat for 1 minute to allow it to heat up and the pores of the metal to open. Pour about 3 tablespoons oil into the wok. As the oil heats, add the scallions and use a wok spatula to push the scallions up along the sides of the wok. The long edges of the scallions will spread the oil around the pan and up the sides without the need for you to tilt the wok and, as a bonus, add a nice fragrance to the oil that is seeping in. As an alternative, if you don't have scallions, grasp strong paper towels with a pair of long tongs and use the towels to carefully spread the oil up the sides. Allow the oil to heat until it is smoking, 5 to 10 minutes. Turn off the heat and allow the wok to cool slightly. Being careful not to touch the wok with your hands, use paper towels to wipe up the excess oil from the inside of the wok. Discard the browned scallions and paper towels.

3. Repeat step 2 three or four times, until the center of the wok has a shiny, dark brown patina. Allow the wok to cool to room temperature, then store in a cool, dry place. The dark brown

spot is the initial layer of seasoning, after the oil has been absorbed into the metal's pores. The more you cook with your wok, the larger and darker the spot will grow. Woks that have been used for years or decades will have a thick black patina that covers the entire wok.

caring for your wok

- Woks are supposed to be a tiny bit oily, so the best way to store them is hanging from a pot rack or in a cupboard with the lid on. Avoid nesting it in any other pans or stacking anything on top.
- In the first few weeks of using your wok, avoid using it to simmer acidic foods like tomatoes (a splash of vinegar is okay if it's mixed with a sauce). This can break down the seasoning of the wok.
- Clean your wok as soon as possible after cooking so food doesn't stick. On the stove top or in the sink, wipe the inside with hot water and a clean sponge that doesn't have soap debris. The hot water should release any remaining food particles.
- To get rid of stubborn food particles on a newly seasoned wok, such as accidentally burned food, rub the insides of the wok with a paper towel and a tiny bit of coarse salt and vegetable oil; the salt will scrub off any stuck-on residue. In addition to the method above, with well-seasoned woks that have developed a thick patina (at least six months of regular use), you can use a tiny bit of soap on a sponge, if needed.
- Never put your wok in the dishwasher.
- After washing, dry your wok thoroughly to prevent rusting. Heat the wok on the stove over high heat until all the water beads have evaporated (no more than 1 to 2 minutes). Allow it to cool before storing it away.
- If a well-meaning spouse or roommate tries to clean your wok by scrubbing it with soap, don't fret; it can be easily reseasoned by following the steps in Seasoning a Wok (page 20). If the wok has rusted, first rub the insides with steel wool or a bit of vegetable oil and coarse salt, which will pick up any grime and rust, before reseasoning.

clockwise from top left: wok ring, bamboo steamer set, microplane grater, mortar and pestle, and julienne peeler

2

appetizers

cold sesame noodles

Starting in the late 1960s, Sichuan restaurants took New York (and later the rest of the country) by storm. A standby appetizer—cold noodles coated with sesame paste and peanut butter, and spiked with chili—became one of the most beloved Chinese dishes in the city. With this recipe, you can make the same savory-sweet noodles you love from the Chinese takeout, with less grease and no MSG. The best noodles to use are Chinese egg noodles or spaghetti; they hold their firmness best and allow the sauce to coat the noodles instead of seeping in. They should be round and not too thin or too thick (the width of a spaghetti strand is perfect). A pinch of spicy Sichuan pepper enhances the flavor of the noodles, but you can certainly leave it out. The velvety noodles are as satisfying freshly made as they are eaten from the fridge at 3:00 a.m.

serves 6 as an appetizer

1. Bring a large pot of water to a boil and cook the noodles until al dente, or the minimum amount of time according to package instructions. Drain immediately, rinse with cold water, and drain again. Put the noodles back into the original pot or a large bowl, toss with 1 tablespoon of the peanut oil, and set aside.

2. In a small dry pan, toast the sesame seeds for about 1 minute, or until they become lightly brown and aromatic. Transfer to a dish and set aside.

3. Heat the remaining ½ tablespoon peanut oil in a small pan over medium-low heat. Gently cook the garlic and ginger until just fragrant, 30 to 40 seconds. Remove from the heat and set aside.

4. Prepare the sauce: In a medium bowl, combine the tahini, peanut butter, soy sauce, sesame oil, rice vinegar, chili sauce, sugar, and Sichuan pepper (if using). Add the water and whisk until the mixture is smooth. Stir in the cooked garlic and ginger.

5. Pour the sauce over the noodles, add the cucumbers and carrots, and toss. Transfer to a large bowl or deep serving dish and sprinkle the toasted sesame seeds and scallions on top. You can serve the sesame noodles at room temperature or chill in the fridge for 1 to 2 hours before serving.

12 ounces dried Chinese egg noodles or spaghetti

1½ tablespoons peanut or vegetable oil

2 teaspoons white sesame seeds

2 teaspoons minced garlic

2 teaspoons grated fresh ginger

sauce

3 tablespoons tahini or other sesame paste

2 tablespoons smooth peanut butter

2 tablespoons soy sauce

1 tablespoon sesame oil

2 tablespoons white rice vinegar

2 teaspoons chili sauce

2 tablespoons sugar

½ teaspoon ground Sichuan pepper (optional)

3 tablespoons water

1 cucumber, halved, seeded, and julienned

2 carrots, julienned

2 scallions, green parts only, thinly sliced

pork and shrimp egg rolls

This iconic appetizer is so popular that practically every Chinese chef has his or her own version. Although restaurants use deep fryers to cook in volume, you can use a wok or heavy-bottomed pot to fry at home. You also don't need a lot of oil; it's easy to get the same great taste and crisp texture of restaurant egg rolls by shallow frying in an inch of oil. For the filling, you can use just about any meat or vegetable that can be thinly sliced, but the combination of pork, shrimp, cabbage, and shiitake mushrooms remains a classic. Wrappers for egg rolls are available in the refrigerator and freezer sections of Asian markets, and increasingly in many Western supermarkets. If you are using frozen egg roll wrappers instead of fresh, defrost them at room temperature for 40 to 50 minutes, or overnight in the refrigerator, before using.

makes 24 egg rolls, serves 6 to 8 as an appetizer

1. Heat a wok or large skillet over medium-high heat until a bead of water sizzles and evaporates on contact. Add 1 tablespoon peanut oil and swirl to coat the bottom. Add the garlic and ginger and stir-fry until just fragrant, about 30 seconds. Add the pork and shrimp and stir-fry for about 2 minutes. Add the cabbage and shiitake mushrooms and continue stir-frying until the vegetables have softened slightly, 1 to 2 minutes.

2. Stir in the soy sauce, sesame oil, sugar, salt, and pepper. Cook until both the shrimp and pork are cooked through, another 2 to 3 minutes. Transfer everything to a shallow bowl and allow to cool for 10 to 15 minutes.

3. When the meat and vegetables are cool enough to handle, strain in a colander or mesh strainer and discard the excess liquid.

4. Fill a small dish with water and place it beside you for sealing the egg rolls later. Have a slightly damp towel or plastic wrap handy to cover the wrappers to prevent the edges from drying and cracking. Take the wrappers from the package as you use them.

5. If the wrappers are stuck together, gently peel them apart to separate. Lay one wrapper on a clean, dry surface, with one corner facing you. Spoon 2 teaspoons of filling onto the wrapper, about 2 inches from the bottom corner (photo 1).

Peanut or vegetable oil for shallow frying

2 teaspoons minced garlic

2 teaspoons grated fresh ginger

8½-pound pork tenderloin, sliced into 2-inch-long matchsticks

½ pound large shrimp, peeled, deveined, and coarsely chopped

2 cups shredded napa cabbage

8 fresh shiitake mushrooms, caps thinly sliced

2 tablespoons soy sauce

1 teaspoon sesame oil

2 teaspoons sugar

½ teaspoon salt

½ teaspoon freshly ground black pepper

24 6-inch Asian egg roll or spring roll wrappers

special equipment

Instant-read oil thermometer

continued

6.   Fold the bottom corner over the filling and begin rolling until you reach halfway up the wrapper (photo 2).

7.   Fold the left and right corners toward the center (photo 3).

8.   Dip your finger in the water and moisten the left and right edges of the top corner. Continue rolling up the wrapper, keeping the left and right edges tucked, to tightly enclose the filling. Seal the roll with the top moistened corner (photo 4).

9.   Lay the finished roll, seam side down, on a dry plate or baking sheet. Keep the finished egg rolls loosely covered with a damp towel or plastic wrap while you repeat the process with the remaining egg rolls.

10.   To fry the egg rolls, fill a wok or heavy-bottomed pot with 1 inch of peanut oil. Heat the oil until it registers 350°F on an instant-read oil thermometer. Gently lower the egg rolls into the oil, frying 3 or 4 at a time, turning them occasionally with tongs or a slotted spoon so that they cook all around, until golden brown, 3 to 5 minutes. Transfer to a plate lined with paper towels to drain and cool.

11.   Repeat the frying process with the remaining egg rolls. Once all the egg rolls have cooled for 5 to 10 minutes, transfer to a serving plate and serve with chili sauce, plum sauce, duck sauce, or Soy and Vinegar Dipping Sauce (page 176).

the pastrami egg roll

Eden Wok in Manhattan is one of the handful of kosher Chinese restaurants around New York that serves the pastrami egg roll. On the outside it looks like an ordinary fried egg roll. On the inside, instead of pork or shrimp, there is pastrami and cabbage, sandwich fillings straight from a Lower East Side deli. This clever mashup of a Jewish deli staple and a Chinese takeout standard shows you don't need pork or shellfish to make a fine egg roll. But do dip it in mustard instead of duck sauce.

classic barbecued spareribs

Barbecued spareribs were the go-to appetizer on Chinese menus in the 1950s and 1960s. Who could resist succulent pork ribs with a sweet and tangy sauce, individually portioned for nibbling? The easiest way to make these barbecued spareribs at home is by roasting them in the oven with an occasional basting with the marinade. The combination of honey, dark soy sauce, hoisin sauce, and ketchup gives this dish a nice tanginess and the reddish, lacquered look of restaurant barbecue, without any food coloring. Dark soy sauce, which is aged and slightly thicker than regular soy sauce, adds more color and a richer flavor to your ribs, but you can always use regular. To make smaller, bite-size spareribs, you can substitute baby back ribs and roast them for 40 minutes instead of 60, with the same amount of broiling time at the end.

serves 4 to 6 as an appetizer

1. Marinate the spareribs: In a small bowl, combine the honey, rice wine, ketchup, hoisin sauce, dark soy sauce, sesame oil, garlic, and five-spice powder. Transfer half of the marinade to another bowl to be used later for basting. Place the spareribs in a large bowl or pan, add the marinade from the first bowl, and toss to coat. Cover with plastic wrap and allow the ribs to marinate in the refrigerator for 1 to 2 hours. Refrigerate the reserved marinade.

2. Preheat the oven to 375°F with one rack on the oven's middle rung. Line a large baking pan with aluminum foil.

3. Once the ribs have marinated, lay them in the baking pan, meat side down. Roast for 60 minutes, using a pastry brush to baste with the reserved marinade every 20 minutes, until the ribs are cooked through. Baste the ribs again, then turn on the broiler. Broil for 5 to 6 minutes, or until the ribs have a nice reddish-brown crust on top. Transfer to a plate. Serve the ribs alone or with Chinese mustard; they taste fantastic either way.

marinade

3 tablespoons honey

2 tablespoons Chinese rice wine or dry sherry

2 tablespoons ketchup

1 tablespoon hoisin sauce

1 tablespoon dark soy sauce

1 teaspoon sesame oil

2 tablespoons minced garlic

½ teaspoon Chinese five-spice powder

2½ pounds pork spareribs, preferably St. Louis style, cut into individual ribs

crab rangoon

Crab Rangoon is widely believed to have been the brainchild of Victor Bergeron, the creator of Trader Vic's, in 1950s San Francisco. He claimed these deep-fried wontons—stuffed with a filling of cream cheese, scallions, and crab—came from an old Burmese recipe, hence the reference to Rangoon, the old name for Burma's capital (today the country is officially Myanmar and its capital, Yangon). Given the absence of cream cheese in Southeast Asian cooking, the claim is highly unlikely, but it fits with Bergeron's persona and penchant for inventing exotic-seeming origins for his restaurant foods. Make this dish at home to ensure your appetizer lives up to its name and contains plenty of crabmeat with every bite. The filling should have a high crab–to–cream cheese ratio; you want the cream cheese flavor to come through, but not make the filling too liquidy. The sweet, delicate flavor of the crab, the richness of the cream cheese, not to mention the satisfyingly crisp exterior, will make this a bona fide favorite at your next party.

makes about 24 wontons, serves 6 as an appetizer

1. Drain the crabmeat and pick it over for shell fragments. (Be sure to drain the crabmeat well, so that when it is mixed with the cream cheese, the mixture does not become too watery.)

2. In a medium bowl, combine the cream cheese and crabmeat. Mix in the scallions, Worcestershire sauce, soy sauce, sesame oil, and salt.

3. On a flat surface, lay out a wonton wrapper with one corner pointed toward you. Drop 2 teaspoons of filling into the center. Wet the edges of the wrapper with a little water. Fold the top corner down to meet the bottom corner, forming a triangle, and gently press out any air. Press the edges together to seal. Set the finished crab rangoon on a plate under a barely damp towel while you repeat the process with the remaining wrappers and filling.

4. Heat 1 inch of peanut oil in a wok or heavy-bottomed pot until the oil registers 350°F on an instant-read oil thermometer. Carefully lower the crab rangoon into the oil, frying 5 or 6 at a time. Fry, turning them over once, until they are golden brown on both sides, about 3 minutes. Remove with a slotted spoon and drain on a plate lined with paper towels. Let the crab rangoon cool for 5 minutes before serving. Serve alone or with soy sauce or plum sauce.

6 ounces cooked lump crabmeat or canned crabmeat

2 tablespoons cream cheese

2 scallions, green parts only, thinly sliced

1 teaspoon Worcestershire sauce

1 teaspoon soy sauce

1 teaspoon sesame oil

¼ teaspoon salt

½ package wonton wrappers (about 24)

Peanut or canola oil for shallow frying

special equipment

Instant-read oil thermometer

shrimp toasts

This seemingly odd concoction of Asian-accented shrimp paste spread over American sandwich bread is actually based on a Cantonese dim sum dish that originated in China more than 100 years ago. The mousse requires no whipping; just a minute in the food processor and it still comes out airy and almost buttery. The water chestnuts add a refreshing crispness to the creamy mousse. Make sure to fry the toasts shrimp side down, so that the shrimp gets fully cooked and the bread does not absorb too much oil. Shrimp Toasts make for great finger foods for your next party.

makes 20 toasts, serves 6 to 8 as an appetizer

1. Trim the crusts off the bread and cut each slice in half into 2 triangles, then in half again to form 4 triangles.

2. Place the water chestnuts in a food processor and pulse until finely chopped. Add the shrimp, egg, cornstarch, rice wine, sesame oil, ginger, sugar, and salt. Pulse until the mixture forms an airy paste, then transfer to a bowl. Stir in the scallions.

3. Spread a thin layer of the shrimp mousse on one side of each triangle of bread. Sprinkle sesame seeds on top of the mousse.

4. To fry the shrimp toasts, fill a wok with 1 inch of peanut oil. Heat the oil until it registers 350°F on an instant-read oil thermometer. Gently lower the triangles into the oil, shrimp side down, and fry until golden, 1 to 2 minutes. Flip over the triangles and fry for about 30 seconds more, until golden. Remove with a slotted spoon and drain on a plate lined with paper towels. Let the toasts cool for 2 minutes, then serve.

5 slices white sandwich bread

4 ounces canned water chestnuts, drained

½ pound large shrimp, peeled and deveined

1 large egg

2 teaspoons cornstarch

1 teaspoon Chinese rice wine or dry sherry

½ teaspoon sesame oil

½ teaspoon grated fresh ginger

½ teaspoon sugar

¼ teaspoon salt

2 scallions, minced

Sesame seeds for garnish

Peanut or vegetable oil for shallow frying

special equipment

Food processor

Instant-read oil thermometer

scallion pancakes

Ideally, scallion pancakes are thin, not too oily, and have flaky layers and a generous sprinkling of chopped scallions. There are few ingredients to the recipe, and most are pantry staples. Once you get used to rolling out the dough, these will easily become part of your appetizer repertoire. And after you coax the dough into little patties, they can be refrigerated or frozen for future use. Also, note that the amount of water needed for the dough can vary if your environment is very humid, whether you live in a tropical climate, or if it's just a rainy day. The best type of pan to use for panfrying is a well-seasoned cast-iron pan or a large skillet; it's possible to use a wok, but the sloping angles make it difficult to fry the pancakes evenly.

makes 6 to 8 pancakes, serves 6 as an appetizer

1. Oil a large mixing bowl and set aside.
2. In a separate large bowl, mix together the flour and water until a smooth dough forms. If the dough seems sticky, as it tends to do in humid weather, add a little more flour (starting with 1 tablespoon and up to ¼ cup total, if needed) and mix again until the dough is no longer sticky.
3. Roll out the dough on a lightly floured work surface and knead for 5 minutes. Place the dough in the greased mixing bowl and turn until it is lightly covered with oil all around. Cover the dough with a barely damp towel and let it rest for 30 minutes.
4. Flour your work surface again and roll out the rested dough. Divide the dough in half, then roll each half into a 1-inch-thick cylinder. With a pastry scraper or butter knife, slice the dough into 2-inch-long segments. Dust your rolling pin with flour and roll out each segment into a 5-inch circle.
5. Lightly brush the top of each circle with peanut oil, about 2 tablespoons total for all the pancakes. Sprinkle with the scallions and salt (photos 1 and 2).
6. Roll up each circle into another cylinder, making sure the scallions stay in place (photos 3 and 4).
7. Coil the dough so that it resembles a snail (photo 5).
8. With a rolling pin, flatten again into disks ¼ inch thick (photos 6 and 7). The pancakes will get a little oily from the

1½ cups all-purpose flour,
plus more if necessary

½ cup warm water

3 tablespoons peanut or vegetable oil,
plus more as needed

3 scallions, thinly sliced

1 teaspoon salt

continued

scallions popping through the dough. Place the rolled-out pancakes on a plate and repeat with the remaining dough. If you stack the pancakes, put a piece of parchment paper between each layer to prevent sticking. (Whatever you don't cook immediately can be frozen for future use.)

9. Heat a nonstick flat-bottomed skillet or cast-iron skillet over medium-high heat and add the remaining 1 tablespoon oil. Working in batches, panfry the pancakes until golden brown, 2 to 3 minutes on each side. If the sides or middle puff up during cooking, press them down with a spatula to ensure even cooking. (You may also need another tablespoon of oil between batches.) Transfer the pancakes to a plate, cut into wedges, and serve, either alone or with chili sauce or Soy and Vinegar Dipping Sauce (page 176) on the side.

pork and mushroom dumplings

for photo see page 24

A perpetual favorite for snacks or meals, dumplings are fun to make at home and easily adaptable to suit your cravings. A favorite combination for the filling is pork and mushrooms, with the richness of the pork complementing the earthiness of the mushrooms. But feel free to vary the ingredients. Pork and cabbage is a Beijing classic, while lamb with leeks is popular in western China. If you love seafood, try shrimp and crab. For vegetarians, spinach with mushrooms and scallions makes an incredibly tasty combination (see Vegetable Dumpling and Wonton Filling, page 41). As for dipping sauces, you can use soy sauce or Sriracha sauce alone, or make the Soy and Vinegar Dipping Sauce (page 176). Once you have the basics down, there is plenty of room to experiment. Any dumplings you don't cook right away can be frozen for a quick meal or snack later on. They can also be panfried or boiled straight out of the freezer; just add 1 minute to the boiling time or steaming part of the panfrying. Follow the step-by-step photographs on page 40 for the secrets to perfect pleating.

makes about 50 dumplings, serves 8 to 10 as an appetizer

1. Make the filling: Soak the shiitake mushrooms in warm water for 15 to 20 minutes. Drain and squeeze out the excess water. Discard the stems and finely chop the mushroom caps.

2. In a large bowl, mix together the mushrooms, pork, scallions, soy sauce, rice wine, sesame oil, salt, and pepper. Set aside.

3. Keep the wrappers covered with a slightly damp towel until ready to use, to prevent them from drying out. Fill a ramekin or small bowl with water and have it next to you; this will be for sealing the dumplings. Take a wrapper and place 1 heaping teaspoon of filling in the middle. Be careful not to put in too much or else it will leak out during the folding process.

4. Dip your finger in the water and moisten the wrapper edges all around. Take the dumpling in your hand and fold the wrapper in half without sealing it. With your right thumb and index finger, make a pleat in the center of the top layer of the wrapper, leaving the bottom layer unpleated (photo 1).

5. Make 2 more identical pleats in the same direction, until you end up with 3 pleats on the right side (photo 2). With your left

filling

8 dried shiitake mushrooms

1 pound ground pork

2 scallions, finely chopped

1 tablespoon soy sauce

1 tablespoon Chinese rice wine or dry sherry

1 tablespoon sesame oil

¼ teaspoon salt

⅛ teaspoon freshly ground black pepper

1 package dumpling wrappers (about 50)

Peanut or vegetable oil for panfrying (about 1 tablespoon per dozen)

continued

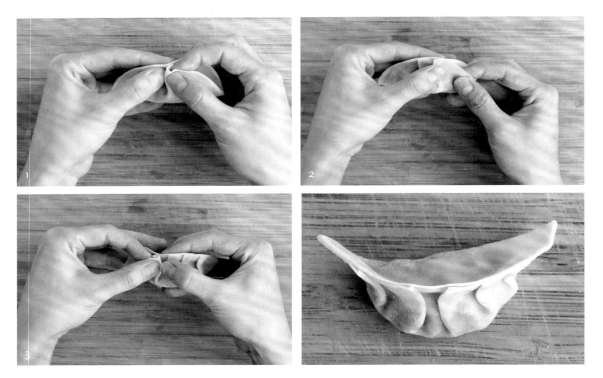

thumb and index finger, make 2 more pleats on the left side (photo 3). Press all the pleats to seal. The finished wrapped dumpling should resemble a crescent.

6.   Lay the finished dumpling on a plate. Keep the dumplings covered with a slightly damp towel while you repeat the process with the remaining dumplings. (This recipe includes instructions for panfrying, but if you would rather boil your dumplings, omit steps 7 through 9 and just cook them in a pot of boiling water for 4 to 5 minutes.)

7.   For panfrying, make sure to use a large flat-bottomed skillet or a wok with a wide flat surface area and have a lid ready. Heat the skillet over medium-high heat until a bead of water sizzles and evaporates on contact. Add 1 tablespoon of the peanut oil and swirl to coat the bottom. Working in batches, line the dumplings in the pan, smooth side down. Cook for 1 to 2 minutes, or until the smooth side starts to brown. Lower the heat to medium. Carefully add about ½ cup water to the pan, and immediately cover with a lid to contain the spitting oil. Allow the dumplings to steam for 4 to 5 minutes, or until all or most of the water has evaporated. Remove the lid and loosen the dumplings with a spatula. They should be golden brown on the bottom. Turn off the heat.

9.   If you are doing repeated batches, wash and dry the pan or wipe it out so that there is no residual water when you panfry your next batch. Repeat the panfrying process with the remaining dumplings, adding more oil as necessary, or freeze some for a rainy day. Serve hot with soy sauce, chili sauce, or Soy and Vinegar Dipping Sauce (page 176).

variation: vegetable dumpling and wonton filling

This is a delicious vegetarian alternative to pork dumplings. The same filling can also be used for vegetarian wontons (see Fried Pork and Shrimp Wontons, page 42, and Wonton Soup, page 55).

1. Soak the shiitake mushrooms in warm water for 15 to 20 minutes. Drain and squeeze out the excess water. Discard the stems and finely chop the mushroom caps.

2. Bring a pot of water to a boil and boil the spinach for 1 to 2 minutes, or until wilted but still bright green. Strain the spinach in a colander, rinse under cold water, and strain again. Shake out the excess water and wring the spinach with your hands. Finely chop the spinach.

3. In a large bowl, mix together the mushrooms, spinach, scallions, soy sauce, sesame oil, salt, and pepper. Set aside.

4. Continue with step 3 of Pork and Mushroom Dumplings (page 39).

filling

8 to 10 dried shiitake mushrooms

2 pounds baby spinach

2 scallions, finely chopped

1 tablespoon soy sauce

2 teaspoons sesame oil

¼ teaspoon salt

⅛ teaspoon freshly ground black pepper

1 package (about 50) dumpling wrappers

Peanut or vegetable oil for panfrying (about 1 tablespoon per dozen)

a dumpling by any other name

pot sticker	English term for any panfried dumpling
gyoza	Japanese term for a panfried dumpling
jiaozi	general Mandarin term for crescent-shape dumpling.
guo tie	panfried dumpling. Literally translates into "pan stick." Probably where pot sticker came from.
shui jiao	boiled dumpling
zheng jiao	steamed dumpling
wonton	a very thin-skinned variety of dumpling that is either boiled or fried. The English name comes from the Cantonese word.

fried pork and shrimp wontons

Wontons, if made well with a pillowy texture, live up to their name, which means "swallowing clouds" in Cantonese. In China they are usually served with noodle soup or, in Sichuan province, boiled and doused in a chili sauce. In the United States, we also have the guilty pleasure of deep-fried wontons, as irresistible an appetizer as French fries or popcorn shrimp. Wonton wrappers, which are square, can be found in Asian supermarkets, and increasingly in Western markets. As with egg rolls and dumplings, wontons can be folded ahead of time and frozen (see assembly instructions on page 44). And contrary to what you may believe based on visits to your favorite takeout spot, you don't need a deep fryer or ungodly amounts of oil to make this dish. A wok and about 3 cups of oil are all you need to make these crispy snacks, without the sogginess so typical of delivery wontons. For a vegetarian filling, see Vegetarian Dumpling and Wonton Filling (page 41).

makes 50 wontons, serves 8 as an appetizer

1. Place a large platter or plate near you and keep a slightly damp towel handy to cover your finished wontons so they don't dry out.

2. In a large bowl, combine the pork, shrimp, scallions, and ginger. Add the soy sauce, rice vinegar, salt, and white pepper and mix until everything is well incorporated. The filling should be sticky and slightly wet.

3. Fill a ramekin or small bowl with water and have it next to you; this will be for sealing the wontons. Angle a wonton wrapper so that it faces you like a diamond. Dip your finger in the water and moisten the edges all around. Place 1 heaping teaspoon of filling in the center of the wrapper (photo 1).

4. Form a triangle by folding the bottom tip to the top tip and pinching out as much air as possible (photo 2).

5. Add a dab of water to either of the two side tips and fold them together, so that one overlaps the other. The end result should resemble a boat, with two tips cradling a puff of filling in the middle (photo 3).

continued

basic wontons

1 pound ground pork

½ pound large shrimp, peeled, deveined, and finely chopped

2 scallions, finely chopped

2 teaspoons minced fresh ginger

1 tablespoon soy sauce

2 teaspoons white rice vinegar

¼ teaspoon salt

¼ teaspoon ground white pepper

1 package wonton wrappers (about 50)

3 cups peanut or vegetable oil

special equipment

Instant-read oil thermometer

6. Place the finished wonton on the platter. Keep the finished wontons covered with the damp towel while you repeat the process with the remaining wontons.

7. To fry the wontons, add the peanut oil to a wok or heavy-bottomed pot. Heat the oil until it registers 350°F on an instant-read oil thermometer. Gently lower the wontons into the oil, frying 6 to 8 at a time for about 4 minutes, while carefully turning with a spatula, until golden brown. Remove the wontons with a slotted spoon and drain on a plate lined with paper towels. Let cool while you finish frying the remaining wontons. Transfer to a plate and serve with soy sauce, chili sauce, or Soy and Vinegar Dipping Sauce (page 176).

hoisin chicken wings

Hoisin sauce, the standard sauce served in China to accompany Peking duck, is also great for marinating and smearing over other roasted meat. Its sweet, garlicky flavor also makes a natural pairing for chicken wings. The process for making these wings couldn't be simpler—just marinate the chicken, shake off the excess liquid before roasting, and baste with the leftover marinade. The wings are sure to be a hit at your next cookout or Super Bowl party.

1. In a large bowl, whisk together the garlic, hoisin sauce, rice vinegar, sesame oil, five-spice powder, cayenne, and salt. Add the wings to the mixture and use your hands to toss and coat the wings with the marinade. Let stand at room temperature for 10 to 15 minutes.

2. Preheat the oven to 400°F. Line a large baking pan with aluminum foil.

3. Remove the wings from the marinade, shaking off the excess and saving marinade for basting. Arrange the wings in a single layer on the baking pan. Roast for 20 minutes. Remove from the oven, baste the wings with the leftover marinade, and sprinkle the sesame seeds (if using) over the wings. Return the wings to the oven and roast for another 10 to 15 minutes, or until the outsides are golden brown and crispy. Transfer to a platter and serve.

marinade

2 garlic cloves, minced

½ cup hoisin sauce

2 tablespoons white rice vinegar

1 teaspoon sesame oil

1 teaspoon Chinese five-spice powder

1 teaspoon cayenne pepper

¼ teaspoon salt

2 pounds chicken wings, drumsticks and wingettes separated

1 teaspoon white sesame seeds (optional)

taiwanese-style pork belly buns

Taiwanese communities in the United States have been feasting on pork belly buns since long before David Chang's Momofuku restaurant empire made them popular in New York. Here, the pork belly is first seared in the pan, then braised with soy sauce, star anise, cinnamon, Sichuan pepper, and chili until it practically melts in your mouth. Peanuts and cilantro are the classic toppings, and you can add a dollop of hoisin sauce for more flavor or squirt a little chili sauce on top for some heat. You can find frozen Chinese steamed buns in the freezer section of a Chinese supermarket. Steam the buns according to the package instructions in a bamboo steamer or a wok with a metal steamer insert. Some buns also have directions on how to steam in a microwave.

serves 4 as an appetizer

1. Cut the pork belly into large pieces (2 inches in length) that are still easy to pick up with tongs.

2. Heat a Dutch oven or heavy-bottomed pot over medium-high heat until a bead of water sizzles and evaporates on contact. Add the peanut oil and swirl to coat the bottom. Add the pork and sear on all sides until lightly browned. Add the garlic, ginger, and scallions and cook briefly, for about 20 seconds, so that they become aromatic.

3. Add the chicken stock, soy sauce, rice wine, sugar, cinnamon, star anise, chilies, and Sichuan pepper. Bring the liquid to boil, then reduce the heat to a simmer. Cover and simmer for 40 to 50 minutes, until the pork belly is fork tender.

4. When the pork is ready, use tongs to transfer it to a cutting board and cut into 1/3-inch-thick slices. Return the pork to the braising liquid and cover to keep warm until the buns are ready.

5. Steam the buns according to package instructions. You can assemble the buns by placing a slice of pork belly on the bottom, then top it off with a small spoonful of hoisin sauce, a dusting of crushed peanuts, and a bit of cilantro. Or for a more hands-on experience for your guests, bring the individual components to the table so that all can assemble their own buns.

1 pound pork belly, preferably boneless with skin on

1 tablespoon peanut or vegetable oil

3 garlic cloves, smashed

1 1-inch piece fresh ginger, peeled and sliced

2 scallions, cut into 2-inch lengths

4 cups Chicken Stock (page 172)

2 tablespoons soy sauce

2 tablespoons Chinese rice wine or dry sherry

2 tablespoons sugar

1 large piece cinnamon stick or cassia bark

2 pieces star anise

2 dried red chilies

1 teaspoon ground Sichuan pepper

1 package large steamed buns (6) or small steamed buns (12)

3 tablespoons hoisin sauce for serving

¼ cup crushed peanuts

Fresh cilantro sprigs

3

soups & salads

egg drop soup

With its steaming chicken broth and wispy egg strands, this soup is a perennial favorite that you will reliably find on the menu at almost every Chinese restaurant. And it's also adaptable: You can easily turn egg drop soup into a hearty meal by adding leftover cooked chicken, pork, or tomatoes and other vegetables.

serves 4 as an appetizer

1. Soak the shiitake mushrooms in warm water for 15 to 20 minutes. Drain and squeeze out the excess water, discard the stems, and thinly slice the mushroom caps.

2. Combine the mushrooms, chicken stock, rice wine, and ginger in a medium pot and bring to a boil. Reduce the heat to a simmer and stir in the sugar, salt, and white pepper.

3. Add the cornstarch mixture to the simmering soup and stir until the soup has slightly thickened—enough to coat the back of a spoon.

4. In a small bowl, whisk the egg lightly with a fork. Slowly pour the egg into the soup in a steady stream while continuously stirring with a long spoon or chopstick. The egg should cook immediately and look like long yellowish-white strands. Turn off the heat after you see the white strands to prevent the egg from overcooking. Ladle the soup into individual bowls, sprinkle the scallions on top, and serve.

6 dried shiitake mushrooms

6 cups Chicken Stock (page 172) or Vegetable Stock (page 173)

1 teaspoon Chinese rice wine or dry sherry

½ teaspoon grated fresh ginger

1 teaspoon sugar

½ teaspoon salt

¼ teaspoon ground white pepper

1 tablespoon cornstarch, dissolved in 3 tablespoons water

1 large egg

1 scallion, green part only, thinly sliced

hot and sour soup

Hot and sour soup is claimed by both Beijing and Sichuan as a regional dish. It's no surprise, then, that the soup became suddenly popular in the 1960s and 1970s, when American diners started to try Chinese dishes beyond the now-familiar Cantonese. The best versions of hot and sour soup have lily buds, shiitake mushrooms, and bamboo shoots that make it a nutrient-rich and even somewhat refined dish. The "hot" comes from the white pepper and the "sour" from a healthy splash of vinegar. The amount of pepper and rice vinegar here is enough to make the soup sufficiently flavored, without being overwhelming, but feel free to adjust the amounts if you would like more bite and tang. As a finishing touch, take a cue from northern China, where diners will drizzle up to a tablespoon of sesame oil over their hot and sour soup. Just a few extra drops will add a wonderful nutty fragrance to your soup.

serves 4 to 6 as an appetizer

1. Soak the shiitake mushrooms and lily buds in warm water for 15 to 20 minutes. Drain and squeeze out the excess water. Slice the stems off the mushrooms and discard. Thinly slice the mushroom caps. Slice the rough black ends off the lily buds and discard, cut the buds in half, and pull apart the strands.

2. Rinse the bamboo shoots and slice them into matchsticks.

3. Drain and rinse the tofu, then drain again. Cut it into ½-inch cubes.

4. In a medium pot, bring the vegetable stock to a boil. Add the mushrooms, lily buds, and bamboo shoots. Simmer for 5 minutes. Carefully add the tofu so that the broth does not splash. Stir in the soy sauce, rice vinegar, Chinese black vinegar, sugar, sesame oil, white pepper, and salt. Simmer for another 3 minutes. Adjust the seasoning with more salt, if needed.

5. Stir in the cornstarch mixture. The soup will become slightly thickened.

6. In a small bowl, whisk the egg lightly with a fork. Slowly pour the egg into the soup in a steady stream while continuously stirring with a long spoon or chopstick. The egg should cook immediately and look like long yellowish-white strands. Turn off the heat after you see the strands so the egg doesn't overcook. Ladle the soup into individual bowls, drizzle a few more drops of sesame oil on top, and serve.

6 dried shiitake mushrooms

4 dried lily buds

¼ cup canned bamboo shoots

½ pound firm tofu

6 cups Vegetable Stock (page 173)

2 tablespoons soy sauce

¼ cup white rice vinegar

1 tablespoon Chinese black vinegar, or substitute good-quality balsamic vinegar

2 teaspoons sugar

2 teaspoons sesame oil, plus more for drizzling

1 teaspoon ground white pepper, or substitute ½ teaspoon ground black pepper

¼ teaspoon salt, plus more to taste

1 tablespoon cornstarch, dissolved in 3 tablespoons water

1 large egg

wonton soup

American diners have been enjoying wonton soup for nearly as long as they have been visiting Chinese restaurants. The soup has transitioned easily from chop suey houses to Polynesian eateries to elegant banquet halls. In New York and California in the 1950s and 1960s, restaurant owners even described wontons as "Chinese kreplach" on menus, a nod to the Jewish clientele who made up a good portion of their customers on both coasts. While wonton soup may be a staple at your corner Chinese takeout, you can make a much tastier version at home without worrying about MSG content. The wontons are the same that you would make for frying (see Fried Pork and Shrimp Wontons, page 42). (In fact, there will be extra wontons left to freeze for later, or to fry.) As for the soup, you can simply use store-bought or homemade chicken stock to great effect, but taking the extra quick-and-simple step to simmer some dried shrimp (see page 13) in the broth adds a nice seafood aroma and flavor.

serves 4 to 6 as an appetizer, or 2 to 3 as a main course

1. Make the wontons as directed.
2. In a medium pot, bring the chicken stock to a boil, then reduce to a simmer. Add the dried shrimp and ginger and simmer for about 20 minutes; the broth should have a faint but pleasant briny aroma at the end. Remove and discard the dried shrimp. Season the broth with salt and white pepper to taste.
3. Add the bok choy to the stock and simmer for another 2 to 3 minutes, or until just cooked. Remove the bok choy and set aside.
4. Bring a large pot of water to a boil. Add the wontons and boil for 4 to 5 minutes, or until the wontons are cooked through. (Trick of the trade: When dumplings float to the top, that usually means they're done, unless the air was not fully squeezed out of the wontons during folding.) Cut one open to check for doneness.
5. Ladle the broth into individual bowls and spoon the bok choy into each. Add the wontons to the bowls, sprinkle the scallions on top, and serve.

½ recipe Basic Wontons (page 42)

2 quarts Chicken Stock (page 172)

2 ounces dried shrimp

1 1-inch piece fresh ginger, peeled and sliced

Salt and ground white pepper

½ pound baby bok choy, washed and chopped

2 scallions, green parts only, thinly sliced

chicken and sweet corn soup

The natural creaminess from corn creates the velvety texture of this soup. The soup is heartier than it seems and takes only 15 to 20 minutes to both prepare and cook. The soup is also a good way to use up leftover roast chicken. Just shred the leftovers (you will need about 2 cups of shredded chicken) and boil the chicken in the soup for 1 to 2 minutes instead of 5.

serves 4 as an appetizer, or 2 as a main course

1. Bring the chicken stock to a boil in a medium pot. Reduce the heat to a simmer and stir in the creamed corn. Add the chicken and cook for about 5 minutes, until the chicken turns white and is cooked through.

2. Add the sesame oil, then add the salt and white pepper. Taste and adjust the seasoning, if necessary. Slowly pour the egg into the soup in a steady stream while continuously stirring with a long spoon or chopstick. The egg should cook immediately and look like long yellowish-white strands. Turn off the heat after you see the strands so the egg doesn't overcook. Ladle the soup into individual bowls and serve.

6 cups Chicken Stock (page 172)

One 14- to 16-ounce can creamed corn

1 boneless, skinless chicken breast, cut into ½-inch cubes

½ teaspoon sesame oil

½ tablespoon salt

¼ teaspoon ground white pepper

1 large egg, beaten

tofu and spinach soup

This light, healthy soup pairs well with any main dish. The number of ingredients is minimal, which is why it is important to use good-quality chicken or vegetable stock, preferably homemade.

serves 4 as an appetizer

1. Bring the chicken or vegetable stock to a boil in a medium pot. Add the ginger, scallion whites, and tofu and cover with a lid. Simmer for 2 to 3 minutes, or until the tofu is heated through.

2. Add the spinach, stirring gently to avoid breaking up the tofu. Season to taste with salt and white pepper. Simmer for about another minute, until the spinach is wilted but not over-cooked.

3. Remove the soup from the heat, toss in the scallion greens, and drizzle the sesame oil on top. Ladle the soup into individual bowls and serve hot.

6 cups Chicken Stock (page 172) or Vegetable Stock (page 173)

2 teaspoons grated fresh ginger

2 scallions, white and green parts separated, thinly sliced

1 pound (about 1 block) silken or soft tofu, drained, rinsed, and cut into 1-inch cubes

4 ounces fresh spinach, cleaned and trimmed

Salt and ground white pepper

2 teaspoons sesame oil

chinese chicken salad

This version of Chinese chicken salad includes the shredded chicken, wonton crisps, and slivered almonds seen in the salad's earliest days, with the oranges and a peanut and sesame dressing that became a popular addition in the 1980s. This basic chicken salad formula lends itself to many variations. For the slivered almonds you could substitute dry-roasted peanuts, chopped cashews, or sesame seeds. You could add julienned cucumbers or snow peas. Finally, for even faster salad prep, you could use leftover roast chicken and skip step 1. However you toss together your salad, rest assured you're fixing up a dish that has been adapted many times through the decades.

serves 4 as part of a multicourse meal, or 2 as a main course

1. Heat a large skillet over medium heat. Add the peanut oil and swirl to coat the bottom of the pan. Sear the chicken breasts for about 4 minutes on each side, or until the outside starts to turn golden brown. Cut open a breast to check for doneness; the juices should run clear. Remove from the heat and allow the chicken to cool on a plate while you prepare the other ingredients.

2. Peel the clementines, separate into segments, and remove the white membranes (pith).

3. Prepare the dressing: In a medium bowl, combine the peanut oil, cider vinegar, peanut butter, soy sauce, honey, sesame oil, garlic, ginger, salt, and pepper. Whisk until smooth and set aside.

4. Once the chicken breasts have cooled, shred them into bite-size pieces. In a large bowl, toss together the shredded chicken, clementines, romaine, carrots, and almonds.

5. Drizzle the dressing on top of the salad. Garnish with crispy chow mein or wonton toppings and serve.

½ tablespoon peanut or vegetable oil

½ pound boneless, skinless chicken breast, or substitute 2 cups leftover cooked chicken

4 seedless clementines or tangerines

dressing

¼ cup peanut or vegetable oil

¼ cup cider vinegar

3 tablespoons smooth peanut butter

2 tablespoons soy sauce

½ tablespoon honey

1 teaspoon sesame oil

1 garlic clove, minced

½ teaspoon grated fresh ginger

1 teaspoon salt

½ teaspoon freshly ground black pepper

8 ounces romaine lettuce, chopped

1 large carrot, julienned

¼ cup slivered almonds

¼ cup crispy chow mein or crispy wonton toppings

a chinese salad, california style

Chinese Chicken Salad is a dish that has the Southern California imprint branded in every bowl. Which other region of the country could have created an entire meal out of chicken breast, lettuce, and a light sesame-accented dressing, with crispy wontons or chow mein noodles thrown in for good measure? Surely it had to come from a place with a healthy appetite for salads and enough culinary caché to popularize this dish by word of mouth.

The debate over who the mastermind behind the Chinese chicken salad was rages on in Los Angeles. Sylvia Wu, who owned the now-closed Madame Wu's Garden, claims to have created the salad for Cary Grant in the 1960s, after he came to her restaurant rhapsodizing about a great chicken salad he had eaten elsewhere. As the story went, she put a chicken salad with almond slivers and wonton crisps on her menu and continued to tweak it for him over time. Others give the credit to Madame Wong, who not only owned two Chinese restaurants that moonlighted as rock clubs and Hollywood hangouts, but also taught Chinese cooking to such stars as Debbie Reynolds and Barbra Streisand. Meanwhile, recipes for similar salads also appeared in *Sunset* magazine as far back as 1957, and in Chinese food manufacturer La Choy's recipe booklets in the 1940s. The debate will surely continue.

The popularity of Chinese chicken salad surged in the 1980s, when celebrity chef Wolfgang Puck put it on the menu at his restaurant Chinois on Main in Santa Monica, California. These days, it's hard to visit a chain restaurant, such as California Pizza Kitchen or The Cheesecake Factory, without finding Chinese chicken salad on the menu. And many Chinese restaurants in and around L.A. still proudly advertise and serve the salad, a Chinese-Californian hodgepodge that became popular around the country.

Sichuan cucumber salad

for photo see page 48

This refreshing cucumber salad is a Sichuan restaurant staple. It's a crisp, refreshing appetizer as well as an effective palate cleanser between bites of fiery Mapo Tofu (page 123) or Spicy Garlic Eggplant (page 122), in chili oil. Pounding the cucumber slices with a blunt object makes them release more water, thereby becoming firmer and absorbing more flavor. The salad is easy to prepare, but the result tastes more complex than you might expect. The crisp, slick cucumbers are at once garlicky, vinegary, savory, spicy, and sweet, with a noticeable scent of sesame. Consider them delicious instant pickles.

serves 4 as an appetizer

1 large cucumber or 2 medium cucumbers, unpeeled

1 teaspoon salt

1 teaspoon peanut or vegetable oil

1 tablespoon minced garlic

2 teaspoons cider vinegar

1 teaspoon soy sauce

1 teaspoon sesame oil

1 teaspoon sugar

¼ teaspoon crushed red pepper flakes

1.　Cut the cucumbers into quarters lengthwise. Slice or scoop out the seedy middle sections, then cut each quarter in half again. Cut the halves into smaller pieces about 1½ inches long.

2.　Crush the cucumber slices by pounding them once or twice with a kitchen mallet, the blunt edge of a cleaver, or the bottom of a coffee mug. The cucumber might spray some juice, so have paper towels handy.

3.　In a large bowl, toss the cucumbers with salt and let sit for 20 minutes, allowing the salt to draw out excess moisture from the cucumbers.

4.　Heat the peanut oil in a small skillet on medium-low heat. Add the garlic and gently cook until fragrant, 30 to 40 seconds, being careful not to let the garlic burn. Remove from the heat, transfer to a small bowl, and toss with the cider vinegar, soy sauce, sesame oil, sugar, and red pepper flakes.

5.　Drain the cucumbers and get rid of any remaining excess moisture by squeezing the cucumbers in the palms of your hands. Toss with the cider vinegar mixture. Transfer to a plate and serve at room temperature, or chill in the fridge until ready to serve. The salad will keep for up to 3 to 4 days in the fridge.

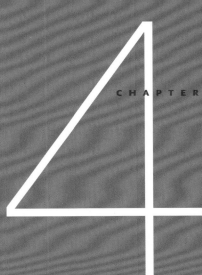

4

chicken & duck

kung pao chicken

This highly addictive stir-fried chicken continues to be one of the most popular Chinese dishes in America as the succulent, complex sauce of salty, sweet, sour, and spicy flavors is hard to pass up. For years Americanized versions often left out the Sichuan peppercorns because of an import ban, but now Sichuan peppercorns are once again easily found in Chinatown shops and even gourmet chains such as Whole Foods.

serves 4 as part of a multicourse meal

1. Marinate the chicken: In a medium bowl, stir together the soy sauce, rice wine, and cornstarch until the cornstarch is dissolved. Add the chicken and stir gently to coat. Let stand at room temperature for 10 minutes.

2. Prepare the sauce: In another bowl, combine the black vinegar, soy sauce, hoisin sauce, sesame oil, sugar, cornstarch, and Sichuan pepper. Stir until the sugar and cornstarch are dissolved and set aside.

3. You may need to turn on your stove's exhaust fan, because stir-frying dried chilies on high heat can get a little smoky. Heat a wok or large skillet over high heat until a bead of water sizzles and evaporates on contact. Add the peanut oil and swirl to coat the base. Add the chilies and stir-fry for about 30 seconds, or until the chilies have just begun to blacken and the oil is slightly fragrant. Add the chicken and stir-fry until no longer pink, 2 to 3 minutes.

4. Add the scallion whites, garlic, and ginger and stir-fry for about 30 seconds. Pour in the sauce and mix to coat the other ingredients. Stir in the peanuts and cook for another 1 to 2 minutes. Transfer to a serving plate, sprinkle the scallion greens on top, and serve.

marinade

1 tablespoon soy sauce

2 teaspoons Chinese rice wine or dry sherry

1½ teaspoons cornstarch

1 pound boneless, skinless, chicken breasts or thighs, cut into 1-inch cubes

sauce

1 tablespoon Chinese black vinegar, or substitute good-quality balsamic vinegar

1 teaspoon soy sauce

1 teaspoon hoisin sauce

1 teaspoon sesame oil

2 teaspoons sugar

1 teaspoon cornstarch

½ teaspoon ground Sichuan pepper

2 tablespoons peanut or vegetable oil

8 to 10 dried red chilies

3 scallions, white and green parts separated, thinly sliced

2 garlic cloves, minced

1 teaspoon minced or grated fresh ginger

¼ cup unsalted dry-roasted peanuts

lemon chicken

In Guangdong province in southern China, lemon chicken means a gently poached chicken breast still on the bone with skin intact, lightly drizzled with lemon juice for flavoring and topped with slices of lemon. It's a perfect dish in hot and humid weather, when all you want is a really light and citrusy entrée. American-Chinese lemon chicken is for all the other times you'd prefer crunchy fried chicken. But while the boneless, skinless chicken is fried, the sweet and tangy lemon sauce—with chicken stock, lemon juice, and lemon zest as the main components—isn't heavy or cloying at all. It's just enough to coat the chicken, so if you would prefer more sauce, just double the sauce ingredients. One of the secrets to getting crispy chicken—for this recipe and for General Tso's Chicken (page 70) and Orange Chicken (page 76)—is to refrain from frying too many pieces at a time, which causes them to steam and prevents them from getting crisp.

serves 4 as part of a multicourse meal

1. Marinate the chicken: In a medium bowl, combine the soy sauce, sesame oil, and egg whites. Add the chicken and stir gently to coat. Let stand at room temperature for 10 minutes.

2. In a small dry pan, toast the sesame seeds for about 1 minute, or until they become lightly brown and aromatic. Transfer to a dish and set aside.

3. Spread the 1½ cups of cornstarch in a large bowl or deep plate. Toss the chicken cubes in the cornstarch and shake off any excess before frying.

4. Heat the peanut oil in a wok or heavy-bottomed pot until it registers 350°F on an instant-read oil thermometer. Carefully add 8 to 10 chicken cubes and deep-fry until lightly golden on the outside and cooked through, about 3 minutes. Remove the chicken with a slotted spoon and drain on a plate lined with paper towels. Repeat with the rest of the chicken. (Optional: To get the chicken extra crispy, allow the chicken to drain and cool for about 5 minutes, then put the chicken back in the wok to fry for about another 30 seconds, until golden brown.)

5. Transfer the oil to a heat-proof container. (It will take about 1 hour to fully cool, after which you can transfer it to a container with a tight lid to dispose of it.) If you used a wok to deep-fry, you

marinade

1 tablespoon soy sauce

1 teaspoon sesame oil

2 large egg whites

1 pound boneless, skinless chicken
    breasts, cut into 1-inch cubes

1 teaspoon white sesame seeds

1½ cups cornstarch

3 cups peanut or vegetable oil,
    plus 1 tablespoon for stir-frying

sauce

2 garlic cloves, minced

1 1½-inch piece fresh ginger, peeled
    and minced

¼ cup Chicken Stock (page 172)

3 tablespoons fresh lemon juice

2 teaspoons grated lemon zest

1 tablespoon soy sauce

2 tablespoons sugar

1 teaspoon cornstarch, dissolved in
    1 tablespoon water

Lemon slices (optional)

can reuse it to make the sauce next by just wiping down the insides with a paper towel. If you used a heavy-bottomed pot for deep-frying, switch to a clean wok or large skillet.

6.   Prepare the sauce: Heat the wok or skillet over medium-high heat until a bead of water sizzles and evaporates on contact. Add the remaining 1 tablespoon peanut oil and swirl to coat the bottom. Add the garlic and ginger and cook briefly until fragrant, about 30 seconds. Add the chicken stock, lemon juice, lemon zest, soy sauce, and sugar. Stir until the sugar is dissolved and simmer until the liquid is reduced by half. Stir in the cornstarch mixture to thicken the sauce.

7.   Remove from the heat and toss the fried chicken in the sauce. Transfer to a serving dish and garnish with the toasted sesame seeds and lemon slices (if using).

special equipment

Instant-read oil thermometer

cashew chicken

Cashew chicken is another takeout favorite that requires less time to cook than to wait for delivery. You can get flavorful chicken by marinating for just 10 to 15 minutes. After allowing the marinade flavors to seep into the meat, the stir-frying takes less than 10 minutes. The recipe calls for salted roasted cashews for the convenience, but if raw cashews are more readily available, just toast them for a minute or two in a small dry pan before adding to the dish.

serves 4 as part of a multicourse meal

1.   Marinate the chicken: In a medium bowl, stir together the soy sauce, rice wine, and cornstarch, until the cornstarch is dissolved. Add the chicken and stir gently to coat. Let stand at room temperature for 10 to 15 minutes.

2.   Prepare the sauce: In a small bowl, mix together the soy sauce, rice wine, oyster sauce, sesame oil, and chili sauce (if using). Set aside.

3.   Heat a wok or large skillet over medium-high heat until a bead of water sizzles and evaporates on contact. Add the peanut oil and swirl to coat the base. Add the garlic and stir-fry until just aromatic, about 20 seconds. Add the marinated chicken and stir-fry for about 2 minutes, until no longer pink on the outside but not yet cooked through.

4.   Add the onions and bell peppers and stir-fry until fragrant and the onions start to become translucent, 1 to 2 minutes.

5.   Pour in the sauce and stir to coat the chicken. Let the sauce simmer for 2 minutes to thicken and allow the chicken to cook through, then stir in the cashews. Transfer to a plate and serve.

marinade

1 tablespoon soy sauce

1 tablespoon Chinese rice wine or dry sherry

1 teaspoon cornstarch

1 pound boneless, skinless chicken breasts or thighs, cut into 1-inch cubes

sauce

2 tablespoons soy sauce

1 tablespoon Chinese rice wine or dry sherry

1 tablespoon oyster sauce

1 teaspoon sesame oil

1 teaspoon chili sauce (optional)

2 tablespoons peanut or vegetable oil

2 garlic cloves, minced

1 medium yellow onion, chopped

1 green bell pepper, chopped

½ cup salted roasted cashews

general tso's chicken

for photo see page 62

When I make General Tso's Chicken, I like to use dark meat, just as the original New York chefs in the 1970s did. Dark meat is juicier and much more tender than white meat and, contrary to widespread belief, not much higher in fat. The sauce, with tomato paste, chicken stock, rice vinegar, and hoisin sauce, thickens up quite nicely in the wok. It's sweet but not overly so, with a mild kick and smoky flavor from the chilies and a good amount of tanginess from the tomato paste and vinegar. Meanwhile, the cornstarch coating results in a brash, proudly crisp exterior. The sauce may taste a little tomato-y on its own, but mixed with the fried chicken it is positively delicious. Left whole, the dried red chilies are not very spicy, but you can split them open and let out the seeds for some more heat. If you prefer your General Tso's chicken on the sweeter side, add an extra 1½ teaspoons of sugar. This recipe makes enough sauce for a light coating; feel free to double the sauce for a heartier dish.

serves 4 as part of a multicourse meal

1. Marinate the chicken: In a large bowl, combine the soy sauce, rice wine, and egg whites. Add the chicken and stir gently to coat. Let stand at room temperature for 10 minutes.

2. In a small dry pan, toast the sesame seeds for about 1 minute, until they become lightly brown and aromatic. Transfer to a dish and set aside.

3. Prepare the sauce: In a small bowl, combine the chicken stock, tomato paste, soy sauce, rice vinegar, hoisin sauce, chili sauce, sesame oil, sugar, and cornstarch. Stir until the sugar and cornstarch are dissolved. Set aside.

4. Toss the 1½ cups cornstarch with the salt and pepper in a large bowl or deep plate. Coat the marinated chicken in the corn-starch mixture and shake off any excess before frying.

5. Heat the peanut oil in a wok or heavy-bottomed pot until it registers 350°F on an instant-read oil thermometer. Working in 2 or 3 batches, add the first batch of chicken cubes and deep-fry until lightly golden on the outside and cooked through, 3 to 4 minutes. Remove the chicken with a slotted spoon and drain on a plate lined with paper towels. Repeat with the rest of the chicken. (Optional: To get the chicken extra crispy, allow the chicken to

marinade

1 tablespoon soy sauce

1 tablespoon Chinese rice wine or dry sherry

2 large egg whites

1 pound boneless, skinless chicken thighs, cut into 1-inch cubes

1 teaspoon white sesame seeds

sauce

¼ cup Chicken Stock (page 172) or water

1½ tablespoons tomato paste

1 tablespoon soy sauce

1 tablespoon white rice vinegar

1 teaspoon hoisin sauce

1 teaspoon chili sauce

1 teaspoon sesame oil

1 tablespoon sugar

1 teaspoon cornstarch

drain and cool for 5 minutes, then put the chicken back in the wok to fry for about another 30 seconds, until golden brown.)

6. Transfer the oil to a heat-proof container. (It will take about 1 hour to fully cool, after which you can transfer it to a container with a tight lid to dispose of it.) If you used a wok to deep-fry, you can reuse it to stir-fry the chicken next by just wiping down the insides with a paper towel. If you used a heavy-bottomed pot for deep-frying, switch to a clean wok or large skillet for stir-frying.

7. Heat the wok or skillet over medium-high heat until a bead of water sizzles and evaporates on contact. Add the remaining 1 tablespoon oil and swirl to coat the bottom. Add the chilies and garlic and stir-fry until just fragrant, about 20 seconds. Pour in the sauce mixture and heat briefly to thicken.

8. Return the chicken to the wok and stir well to coat with sauce. Transfer the chicken to a serving dish. Garnish with the toasted sesame seeds and scallions and serve.

1½ cups cornstarch

½ teaspoon salt

½ teaspoon freshly ground black pepper

3 cups peanut or vegetable oil for frying, plus 1 tablespoon for stir-frying

8 dried whole red chilies, or substitute ¼ teaspoon crushed red pepper flakes

2 cloves garlic, minced

Scallions, green parts only, thinly sliced

special equipment

Instant-read oil thermometer

general tso's: the chicken that conquered america

You may know this dish as General Tso's, General Zuo's, General Joe's, or another variation. Although in one spelling or another, his name graces the menus of tens of thousands of Chinese restaurants around the United States, the real-life Zuo Zongtang was never a chef and never even tasted his namesake chicken dish. He was, in fact, a nineteenth-century general known for squashing military uprisings and one of China's most famed historical figures.

A century later, one of his many admirers was Peng Chang-kuei, a chef from Hunan province who cooked for the Nationalist government during the Chinese civil war. In 1949, to escape the impending Communist takeover, he fled to Taiwan where for two decades he continued his career as a chef. It was in Taiwan that he created a dish of fried spicy and tangy chicken and named it after the famed general. The chicken was not from a standard repertoire of classic Hunan recipes, but its strong flavor components had been characteristic of the province's cooking for centuries.

In the early 1970s, New York was experiencing a renewed love affair with Chinese food and seeking flavors beyond Cantonese cuisine. (This was further fueled by Richard Nixon's historic 1972 trip to China and televised banquet dinner with the Chinese premier.) Two chefs from New York made separate trips to Taiwan looking for inspiration for new regional cuisines and ended up eating at Chef Peng's restaurant. When the chefs returned, they opened Hunan restaurants in New York within weeks of each other, with conspicuously similar menus, including versions of Peng's innovative chicken dish. Both restaurants gained critical and commercial success. By the time Chef Peng arrived in New York and opened his own Hunan restaurant in midtown, his version of Hunan food, including General Tso's Chicken, was no longer groundbreaking. He did, however, continue to reap the benefits of Hunan's popularity, not to mention draw such notable fans as Henry Kissinger, who ate at the restaurant on his frequent trips to New York.

Because General Tso's Chicken was created in Taiwan and made famous in the United States, it's no surprise that few people in Hunan have ever heard of it. However, it still embodies the spirit of Hunan cooking and history, and is a shining example of the inventiveness and legacy of the cultural adaptation of the Chinese in America.

stir-fried sesame chicken

This stir-fry version of sesame chicken is a healthier take on the classic restaurant dish, and requires only 10 minutes or less of hands-on preparation. The chili sauce is optional, for those who prefer their sesame chicken spicier. Pair this chicken with Stir-Fried Asparagus Tips (page 131) or Simple Broccoli Stir-Fry (page 127) for a quick, fresh-tasting dinner.

serves 4 as part of a multicourse meal

1. Marinate the chicken: In a medium bowl, stir together the sesame oil, soy sauce, rice wine, ginger, and cornstarch until the cornstarch is dissolved. Add the chicken and stir gently to coat. Let stand at room temperature for 15 to 20 minutes.

2. In a small dry pan, toast the sesame seeds for about 1 minute, or until they become lightly brown and aromatic. Transfer to a dish and set side.

3. Prepare the sauce: In a separate bowl, stir together the chicken stock, soy sauce, sesame oil, honey, rice vinegar, chili sauce (if using), and cornstarch until the cornstarch is dissolved. Set aside.

4. Heat a wok or large skillet over high heat until a bead of water sizzles and evaporates on contact. Add the peanut oil and swirl to coat the bottom. Add the garlic and stir-fry until aromatic, about 30 seconds. Add the chicken and stir-fry for about 2 minutes, or until no longer pink on the outside but not yet cooked through. Add the frozen peas and cook for 1 minute. Stir in the sauce and let it simmer for 1 to 2 minutes to thicken. Transfer to a serving dish and sprinkle the toasted sesame seeds on top.

marinade

1 tablespoon sesame oil

1½ teaspoons soy sauce

1½ teaspoons Chinese rice wine or dry sherry

1 teaspoon grated fresh ginger

1 teaspoon cornstarch

1 pound boneless, skinless chicken breasts, cut in ¼-inch thick slices

1 teaspoon white sesame seeds

sauce

¼ cup Chicken Stock (page 172)

1 tablespoon soy sauce

1 tablespoon sesame oil

1 tablespoon honey

1 teaspoon white rice vinegar

1 teaspoon chili sauce (optional)

2 teaspoons cornstarch

1 tablespoon peanut or vegetable oil

1 garlic clove, minced

1 cup frozen peas

moo goo gai pan

Moo goo gai pan is a simple chicken stir-fry with button mushrooms and other fresh vegetables. With chicken stock as its main ingredient, the sauce is light in both color and texture, in contrast to the soy-based brown sauce that many takeout dishes have. The best way to enjoy this dish is in front of the TV, feet propped on the coffee table, perhaps watching a sitcom from decades past, where the dish had been featured—remember the *Bob Newhart* Thanksgiving episode, or Laura's favorite Chinese food, "heavy on the goo," on *The Dick Van Dyke Show*.

serves 4 as part of a multicourse meal

1. Marinate the chicken: In a medium bowl, stir together the soy sauce, rice wine, and cornstarch until the cornstarch is dissolved. Add the chicken and stir gently to coat. Let stand at room temperature for 10 minutes.

2. Prepare the sauce: In a small bowl, combine the chicken stock, rice wine, soy sauce, oyster sauce, sugar, and cornstarch. Stir until the sugar and cornstarch are dissolved. Set aside.

3. Heat a wok or large skillet over high heat until a bead of water sizzles and evaporates on contact. Add the peanut oil and swirl to coat the bottom. Add the chicken and stir-fry for about 3 minutes, until it is no longer pink. Remove the chicken with a slotted spoon and set aside.

4. In the same wok, add the garlic and ginger and stir-fry until fragrant, about 30 seconds. Add the snow peas and mushrooms and cook for 3 minutes, stirring occasionally. Return the chicken slices to the wok and stir in the sauce. Let the mixture simmer for 1 to 2 minutes, until the sauce is slightly thickened. Add salt and pepper to taste. Transfer to a plate and serve.

marinade

1½ tablespoons soy sauce

1½ tablespoons Chinese rice wine or dry sherry

1 teaspoon cornstarch

¾ pound boneless, skinless chicken breasts, cut into ¼-inch-thick slices

sauce

¼ cup Chicken Stock (page 172)

1 tablespoon Chinese rice wine or dry sherry

2 teaspoons soy sauce

2 teaspoons oyster sauce

1 teaspoon sugar

1 teaspoon cornstarch

2 tablespoons peanut or vegetable oil

1 teaspoon finely chopped garlic

1 teaspoon finely chopped fresh ginger

4 ounces snow peas, sliced in half

½ pound cremini or white button mushrooms, stems removed and caps quartered

Salt and freshly ground black pepper

orange chicken

Orange chicken gets its name from a more traditional Chinese dish called orange peel chicken or tangerine chicken, whose sauce is flavored with dried tangerine peels. Because dried tangerine peels were often hard to find outside of China, restaurant cooks here in the United States began substituting orange juice and boiling it down to a syrup. The version here combines orange juice and fresh orange zest for a brighter, more citrusy sauce. Sprinkling in a bit of cayenne adds a kick, but you can leave it out if you prefer. As with the Lemon Chicken (page 66), you should refrain from frying too much chicken in the pan at one time, which prevents the nuggets from getting crispy; 8 to 10 pieces at a time in a large wok or heavy-bottomed pot is ideal.

serves 4 as part of a multicourse meal

1. Marinate the chicken: In a large bowl, combine the soy sauce, rice wine, and egg whites. Add the chicken and stir gently to coat. Let stand at room temperature for 10 minutes.

2. Prepare the sauce: In a separate bowl, combine the orange juice, chicken stock, cider vinegar, soy sauce, sesame oil, brown sugar, orange zest, and cayenne (if using). Set aside.

3. Heat the 1 teaspoon of peanut oil in a saucepan over medium heat and sauté the garlic until fragrant, about 1 minute. Add the reserved sauce and bring the mixture to a boil. Reduce the heat to a simmer and allow the sauce to simmer until it is reduced by three fourths, about 15 minutes. Stir in the cornstarch and water mixture until the sauce thickens. Season with salt to taste. Turn off the heat and cover to keep warm.

4. Spread the 1½ cups of cornstarch in a large bowl or deep plate. Toss the marinated chicken in the cornstarch and shake off any excess before frying.

5. Heat the 3 cups peanut oil in a wok or heavy-bottomed pot until it registers 350°F on an instant-read oil thermometer. Carefully add 8 to 10 chicken cubes and fry until lightly golden on the outside and cooked through, 3 to 4 minutes. Remove the chicken with a slotted spoon and drain on a large plate lined with paper towels. Repeat with the rest of the chicken. (Optional: To get the chicken extra crispy, allow the chicken to drain and cool for

marinade

1 tablespoon soy sauce

1 tablespoon Chinese rice wine or dry sherry

2 large egg whites

1 pound boneless, skinless chicken breasts or thighs, cut into 1-inch cubes

sauce

⅓ cup orange juice

¼ cup Chicken Stock (page 172)

1 tablespoon cider vinegar

1½ tablespoons soy sauce

1 teaspoon sesame oil

2 tablespoons light brown sugar

1 teaspoon grated fresh orange zest

¼ teaspoon cayenne pepper (optional)

3 cups peanut or vegetable oil for frying, plus 1 teaspoon for sautéing

1 garlic clove, minced

1 teaspoon cornstarch, dissolved in 1 tablespoon water

Salt

1½ cups cornstarch

5 minutes, then put the chicken back in the wok to fry for about another 30 seconds, or until golden brown.)

6. Transfer the oil to a heat-proof container. (It will take about 1 hour to fully cool, after which you can transfer it to a container with a tight lid to dispose of it.)

7. Reheat the orange sauce and stir in the fried chicken cubes. Mix until well coated. Transfer to a plate and serve.

special equipment

Instant-read oil thermometer

the oldest chinese restaurant in america

Curiously, here in the United States, the oldest surviving Chinese restaurant is not in San Francisco, New York, or any other city with a vibrant Chinatown. Instead, it's in Butte, Montana, a historically rough-and-tumble western boomtown, where the current Asian population is about 150 people.

The Pekin Noodle Parlor has been standing on South Main Street since 1916 and is one of the many businesses opened by the Chinese since their arrival in the 1860s. At one time, Butte had a small Chinatown complete with grocery stores, restaurants, tailors, and herbal shops. Over time many Chinese moved east for better job prospects, but somehow the Pekin Noodle Parlor has endured, even staying within the same family ownership. The atmosphere is a throwback to the early twentieth century. Diners must pass under a neon CHOP SUEY sign and climb up a narrow, rickety set of wooden stairs to reach the second-floor restaurant. They sit in curtained pink booths, holdovers from the parlor's former life as a brothel, as the waitstaff brings out food through swinging wooden doors straight out of an old Western. Even the food seems to have remained unchanged for nearly a century; chop suey, chow mein, and egg foo young (see Egg Foo Young with Gravy, page 120), all available in many varieties, are still the most popular items on the menu.

spicy black bean chicken

Fermented black beans have been used as a cooking ingredient in China for even longer than soy sauce. They get their robust earthy aroma and flavor from being dried and salted, then aged in oil, and are frequently used in rustic dishes from Sichuan and Hunan provinces, as well as in Cantonese seafood dishes. Any extra black beans will keep for at least a year if stored in a tightly sealed jar in the back of the refrigerator.

serves 4 as part of a multicourse meal

1.   Marinate the chicken: In a small bowl, stir together the soy sauce, rice wine, and cornstarch until the cornstarch is dissolved. Add the chicken and gently stir to coat. Let stand at room temperature for 10 minutes.

2.   Rinse the black beans to remove any grit. In a small bowl, mash the black beans with the back of a spoon and set aside.

3.   Prepare the sauce: In another small bowl, combine the rice wine, soy sauce, chili oil, cumin, and paprika. Set aside.

4.   Heat a wok or large skillet over high heat until a bead of water sizzles and evaporates on contact. Add the peanut oil and swirl to coat the bottom. Add the chicken and stir-fry until it is no longer pink on the outside but not yet cooked through, 2 to 3 minutes. Add the onions, garlic, ginger, and fermented black beans and stir-fry for another minute.

5.   Add the sauce and scrape the bottom of the wok with a spatula to loosen up any juicy brown bits. Stir to coat the chicken. Simmer until the sauce is slightly thickened, about 1 minute. Transfer to a plate and serve.

marinade

1 tablespoon soy sauce

1 tablespoon Chinese rice wine or dry sherry

2 teaspoons cornstarch

1 pound boneless, skinless chicken breasts, sliced into 1-inch cubes

2 tablespoons fermented black beans

sauce

2 tablespoons Chinese rice wine or dry sherry

2 tablespoons soy sauce

¼ teaspoon chili oil

½ teaspoon ground cumin

½ teaspoon paprika

1 tablespoon peanut or vegetable oil

1 yellow onion, chopped

1 garlic clove, minced

1 teaspoon julienned fresh ginger

pineapple chicken

In the 1940s, if you had a hankering for Chinese food by way of a tropical island, you didn't have to look farther than a tiki restaurant or large Chinatown eatery. The legendary California tiki entrepreneur Don the Beachcomber, who was seemingly infatuated with all things pineapple, put pineapple chicken on his menus as early as 1941, to go with his daiquiris and rum punches. To this day, this sweet and tangy dish still shows up on tiki menus, and Chinese takeout restaurants around the country have adopted it into their repertoire. This dish is great because it gives you a lot of leeway with vegetables. The onions and bell peppers add a little crunch, but you can substitute other quick-cooking vegetables, such as asparagus, broccoli, and snow peas. It's also one of the lightest stir-fries in this book, and the minimal number of ingredients allow the natural flavor of the pineapple to come through.

serves 4 as part of a multicourse meal, or 2 as a main course

1. Marinate the chicken: In a medium bowl, combine the soy sauce, rice wine, and sesame oil. Add the chicken and stir gently to coat. Let stand at room temperature for 10 minutes.

2. Heat a wok or large skillet over medium heat until a bead of water sizzles and evaporates on contact. Add the peanut oil and swirl to coat the bottom. Cook the onions and bell peppers for about 1 minute, until the onions are translucent and aromatic. Add the chicken slices and stir-fry for about 2 minutes, until no longer pink on the outside but not yet cooked through. Stir in the cider vinegar and soy sauce. Add the pineapple and cook for about another 2 minutes (1 minute for canned pineapple). Add salt and pepper to taste. Transfer to a plate and serve.

marinade

1½ teaspoons soy sauce

2 teaspoons Chinese rice wine or dry sherry

½ teaspoon sesame oil

¾ pound boneless, skinless chicken breasts, cut into ¼-inch-thick slices

1 tablespoon peanut or vegetable oil

½ yellow onion, chopped

½ red bell pepper, chopped

2 teaspoons cider vinegar

1 tablespoon soy sauce

1 cup chopped fresh pineapple, tossed in 2 teaspoons sugar, or substitute 1 cup canned pineapple chunks, drained; no need to toss in extra sugar

Salt and freshly ground black pepper

velvet chicken

Velveting is a technique that involves marinating the meat in an egg white–and–cornstarch mixture, then blanching the meat in water or oil before stir-frying. Although velveting is a little bit more time-consuming than regular stir-frying, egg whites mixed with cornstarch provide a great protective layer around the meat or shellfish, so the meat or shellfish retains moisture and remains incredibly tender. In this recipe, stir-fry the chicken briefly until cooked through but not browned, because the blanching has already partially cooked the chicken. Crisp snow peas are great alongside the silky-smooth and mild-flavored chicken.

serves 4 as part of a multicourse meal

1.   In a small bowl, stir together the rice wine and cornstarch until the cornstarch is dissolved; be sure it is fully dissolved or else it can turn clumpy when added to the egg. In a medium bowl, lightly beat the egg white for a few seconds. (It should not be beaten enough to turn frothy.) Add the cornstarch mixture to the beaten egg white and stir until the mixture is dissolved. Add the chicken and stir gently to coat. Cover and let stand in the refrigerator for 30 minutes so that the coating can adhere to the chicken.

2.   Bring the water to a boil in a deep pot or saucepan. Stir in 1 tablespoon of the peanut oil (this will help prevent the chicken slices from sticking to one another), then reduce the heat to a very gentle simmer. With a slotted spoon, carefully add the chicken and lightly stir for about 2 minutes, until the coating is white but the chicken is not yet cooked through. Drain the chicken in a colander and shake out the excess water.

3.   Heat a wok or large skillet over medium-high heat until a bead of water sizzles and evaporates on contact. Add the remaining 1 tablespoon peanut oil and swirl to coat the bottom. Add the garlic and ginger and stir-fry until aromatic, about 30 seconds. Add the snow peas and stir-fry for about 3 minutes, or until crisp-tender and still bright green. Drizzle on the sesame oil and sprinkle the sugar over the snow peas. Add the chicken and stir-fry for another 1 to 2 minutes, or until the chicken is cooked through and still white all around. Add salt and white pepper to taste. Transfer to a plate and serve.

marinade

1 tablespoon Chinese rice wine or dry sherry

2 teaspoons cornstarch

1 large egg white

1 pound boneless, skinless chicken breasts, cut into ¼-inch-thick slices

1 quart water

2 tablespoons peanut or vegetable oil

1 teaspoon minced garlic

1 teaspoon minced fresh ginger

4 ounces snow peas, hard ends trimmed

1 teaspoon sesame oil

½ teaspoon sugar

Salt and ground white pepper

chinatown roast duck

The taste of roast duck brings back fond memories of my childhood in Boston. Every Sunday morning, my mom and I would head down to Chinatown for grocery shopping. We'd walk by shop after shop with freshly roasted ducks hanging in the windows, their lacquered reddish-brown skin glistening enticingly. We usually headed to my mom's favorite butcher, who would package up an especially plump duck for us to take home for Sunday dinner. The hard part was waiting until evening to eat! Every once in a while, if she wasn't too busy, my mom would roast her own duck. The duck needs to be prepared a day in advance, but the effort is well worth it. For this recipe we use precut duck legs for convenience. The important first step is to boil water and pour the hot water over the duck's skin to make it taut and to enlarge its pores, so the marinade seeps in. After overnight marinating comes the air-drying, which makes the skin extra crispy. While restaurant chefs have bigger kitchens in which to hang the ducks to air-dry overnight, my mom taught me to improvise by setting the duck in front of a fan on a roasting rack with a pan underneath to catch drippings. The duck air-dries much more quickly, and the result is still crispy and delicious.

serves 2 to 3 as part of a multicourse meal

1. Use tweezers to remove any remaining quills on the duck's skin.

2. Bring the water to a boil in a pot or kettle. Place the duck legs, skin side up, in a large heatproof colander or mesh strainer over the sink, and pour the hot water over the skin. This will make the skin more taut, without cooking the meat. Rinse the duck under cold water to cool, then transfer to a cutting board and pat dry with paper towels.

3. With the tip of a sharp knife, prick the skin 8 to 10 times per leg, being careful not to prick the flesh. This creates tiny holes that will allow the fat to escape more easily during roasting.

4. Marinate the duck: In a small bowl, combine the soy sauce, honey, rice vinegar, hoisin sauce, ginger, five-spice powder, and white pepper. Brush the duck all over with the marinade. Transfer the duck and the remaining marinade to a gallon-size freezer bag, making sure the duck is well coated. Allow the duck to marinate in the fridge overnight.

5. The following day, set a metal cooling rack over a roasting pan lined with aluminum foil. Remove the duck from the mari-

2 duck legs
1 quart water

marinade

3 tablespoons soy sauce
2½ tablespoons honey
2 tablespoons white rice vinegar or cider vinegar
1 tablespoon hoisin sauce
2 teaspoons grated fresh ginger
½ teaspoon Chinese five-spice powder
½ teaspoon ground white pepper

nade, and place the duck legs on the rack and aim a fan directly at them. Turn the fan to a medium to high setting and air-dry the duck for 1 to 2 hours, rotating occasionally, until the skin dries evenly.

6.   Preheat the oven to 450°F.

7.   Wipe up any grease that may have accumulated in the bottom of the roasting pan while the duck was cooling. Arrange the duck, skin side up, in the pan. Roast for 20 minutes, then baste the skin with the drippings that will have accumulated in the pan. Lower the heat to 400°F and continue to roast for about another 20 minutes, until the skin becomes reddish brown and crispy.

8.   Remove the duck from the oven and allow it to cool for 6 to 8 minutes. Cut into 1-inch-thick slices and serve with hoisin sauce or plum sauce.

5

beef, pork, & lamb

beef with broccoli

In the early 1900s, adapting to their new surroundings, Chinese cooks in America began preparing this dish using Western broccoli, as Chinese broccoli wasn't widely available. With the quick stir-frying time and common pantry ingredients, this is one of the easiest Chinese dishes to make at home. The secret to getting crisp, bright green broccoli is to blanch it first and stir-fry the beef separately. The beef is lusciously tender, thanks to the cornstarch marinade.

serves 4 as part of a multicourse meal

1. Marinate the beef: In a medium bowl, stir together the soy sauce, rice wine, and cornstarch until the cornstarch is dissolved. Add the beef and stir gently to coat. Let stand at room temperature for 10 minutes.

2. Prepare the sauce: In a small bowl, stir together the chicken stock, oyster sauce, soy sauce, rice wine, and cornstarch until the cornstarch is dissolved. Set aside.

3. Bring a large pot of water to a boil. Blanch the broccoli in the boiling water for 2 minutes. (If you want the broccoli to maintain its bright green hue, add ½ teaspoon of baking soda to the boiling water.) Rinse the broccoli under running cold water. Drain thoroughly and set aside.

4. Heat a wok or large skillet over high heat until a bead of water sizzles and evaporates on contact. Add the peanut oil and swirl to coat the bottom. Add the garlic and ginger and stir-fry briefly until fragrant, about 30 seconds. Add the beef and stir-fry until lightly brown on the outside but not yet cooked through, 1 to 2 minutes.

5. Pour in the sauce and bring it to a simmer. Add the blanched broccoli. Continue to cook the beef and broccoli for another minute, stirring so that everything is well coated. Season with pepper to taste. Transfer to a serving dish and serve immediately.

NOTE: When cutting beef, be sure to slice against the grain so that the beef remains tender throughout cooking. Pork and lamb don't have similar tough fibers, so you can slice them in any direction. For any red meat, slicing is easier if you throw it in the freezer for 20 minutes beforehand to harden it a bit.

marinade

2 teaspoons soy sauce

2 teaspoons Chinese rice wine or dry sherry

1 teaspoon cornstarch

¾ pound flank steak, cut against the grain into ¼-inch-thick slices (see Note below)

sauce

¼ cup Chicken Stock (page 172)

2 tablespoons oyster sauce

1½ tablespoons soy sauce

1 tablespoon Chinese rice wine or dry sherry

2 teaspoons cornstarch

3 to 4 cups broccoli florets

2 tablespoons peanut or vegetable oil

2 garlic cloves, minced

1 teaspoon minced or grated fresh ginger

Freshly ground black pepper

pepper steak

Pepper steak has been a mainstay at Chinese restaurants in the United States since the early part of the last century, with its popularity exploding in the 1940s. Midcentury cookbooks, and food sections in newspapers from the *Wisconsin State Journal* to *The New York Times,* printed recipes to show busy home cooks how to make this Chinese restaurant favorite in their own kitchens. And not much has changed since then. The trick to preparing this lightning-fast dish is thinly slicing the beef, bell pepper, and onion. After marinating the beef to make it tender, it takes only a few minutes of stir-frying to get a piping-hot dish of pepper steak on the table

serves 4 as part of a multicourse meal

1. Marinate the beef: In a medium bowl, stir together the soy sauce, rice wine, and cornstarch until the cornstarch is dissolved. Add the beef and stir gently to coat. Let stand at room temperature for 10 minutes.

2. Prepare the sauce: In a small bowl, stir together the chicken stock, soy sauce, rice wine, Worcestershire sauce, ketchup, sesame oil, and sugar. Set aside.

3. Heat a wok or large skillet over high heat until a bead of water sizzles and evaporates on contact. Add 1 tablespoon of the peanut oil and swirl to coat the bottom and sides. Add the beef and stir-fry until the outside is light brown but not yet cooked through, 1 to 2 minutes. Transfer the beef to a plate and set aside.

4. In the same wok, add the remaining 1 tablespoon oil. Add the garlic and ginger and stir-fry briefly until fragrant, about 20 seconds. Add the bell peppers and onions and stir-fry for about 1 minute, until the onions begin to turn translucent. Return the beef to the wok. Swirl in the sauce and cook for another minute, stirring so that everything is well combined. Season with salt and pepper to taste. Transfer to a serving dish and serve immediately.

marinade

2 teaspoons soy sauce

2 teaspoons Chinese rice wine or dry sherry

1 teaspoon cornstarch

¾ pound flank steak, cut against the grain into ¼-inch-thick slices

sauce

2 tablespoons Chicken Stock (page 172)

1 tablespoon soy sauce

1 tablespoon Chinese rice wine or dry sherry

1 tablespoon Worcestershire sauce

1½ teaspoons ketchup

¼ teaspoon sesame oil

1 teaspoon sugar

2 tablespoons peanut or vegetable oil

1 tablespoon minced garlic

1 teaspoon minced or grated fresh ginger

1 green bell pepper, thinly sliced

1 medium yellow onion, thinly sliced

Salt and freshly ground pepper

sichuan dry-fried beef

In Sichuan cooking, there is a method known as dry frying, which involves cooking meat or vegetables over medium heat for a longer period of time than stir-frying, until the ingredients become crispy on the outside but still tender on the inside. Beef is one of the most popular meats to dry fry, while Dry-Fried Green Beans (page 128) is one of Sichuan's most well-known vegetable dishes. This dry-fried beef recipe calls for 8 minutes of frying time. After the beef has cooked, it will look a little like beef jerky, but the taste is actually remarkably succulent. Dry frying also concentrates the flavor of the beef and doesn't result in too much excess oil in the finished dish. Here, the sliced bell pepper provides a crunchy, colorful contrast to the beef.

serves 4 as part of a multicourse meal

1. Prepare the sauce: In a small bowl, combine the rice wine, chili paste, soy sauce, Sichuan pepper, and black pepper. Set aside.

2. Heat a wok or large skillet over medium-high heat until a bead of water sizzles and evaporates on contact. Add 3 tablespoons of the peanut oil, swirl to coat the bottom, and wait for 1 minute for the oil to heat up. Add the beef, spread it out evenly, and allow it to sizzle undisturbed for 1 to 2 minutes. (The oil will become cloudy initially as the beef releases its juices.) Cook the beef for about another 6 minutes, stirring occasionally, until the oil becomes clear again. The beef should be mostly dark brown and, having lost most of its water content, also crispy in texture. Transfer the beef to drain on a plate lined with paper towels.

3. Drain the oil from the wok and wipe the wok clean with a paper towel, being careful not to touch the hot sides with your hands. Swirl in the remaining 1 tablespoon oil. Add the chilies, garlic, and ginger and stir-fry until just aromatic, about 30 seconds. Add the bell peppers and stir-fry for another minute. Return the beef to the wok and pour in the sauce, using a spatula to release any brown bits from the bottom of the wok. Toss in the scallions. Transfer to a plate and serve.

sauce

2 tablespoons Chinese rice wine or dry sherry

1 tablespoon chili paste

1 teaspoon soy sauce

½ teaspoon ground Sichuan pepper

¼ teaspoon freshly ground black pepper

4 tablespoons peanut or vegetable oil

1 pound flank steak, sliced against the grain into ¼-inch-thick slices

4 to 5 dried red chilies

1 garlic clove, minced

1 teaspoon julienned fresh ginger

1 red, orange, or yellow bell pepper, thinly sliced

2 scallions, cut into 3-inch lengths and shredded

mongolian beef

for photo see page 84

This hearty and not too heavy stir-fry is quick and easy—all the sauce ingredients are readily available in your pantry. If you'd like to create an entire meal of northern-style Chinese dishes, try rounding this out with Hot and Sour Soup (page 52) and Yangzhou Fried Rice (page 152).

serves 4 as part of a multicourse meal

1.   Marinate the beef: In a medium bowl, stir together the soy sauce, rice wine, and cornstarch until the cornstarch is dissolved. Add the beef and stir gently to coat. Let stand at room temperature for 10 minutes.

2.   Prepare the sauce: In a small bowl, combine the soy sauce, hoisin sauce, chili sauce, rice wine, oyster sauce, sesame oil, and red pepper flakes. Set aside.

3.   Heat a wok or large skillet over high heat until a bead of water sizzles and evaporates on contact. Add the peanut oil and swirl to coat the bottom. Add the beef and allow it to cook undisturbed for 1 minute so that it begins to sear. Stir-fry for about another minute, or until the beef browns on the outside but is not cooked through. Add the leeks and ginger and stir-fry for about 1 minute, until the leeks begin to wilt. Add the sauce, stirring so that the beef is well coated. Cook until the beef is cooked through, another 1 to 2 minutes. Transfer to a plate, garnish with the shredded scallions, and serve hot.

marinade

1 tablespoon soy sauce

1 tablespoon Chinese rice wine or dry sherry

2 teaspoons cornstarch

1 pound flank steak, cut against the grain into ¼-inch-thick slices

sauce

2 tablespoons soy sauce

2 teaspoons hoisin sauce

2 teaspoons chili sauce

2 teaspoons Chinese rice wine or dry sherry

1 teaspoon oyster sauce

1 teaspoon sesame oil

½ teaspoon crushed red pepper flakes

1 tablespoon peanut or vegetable oil

2 leeks, white part only, thinly sliced

1 teaspoon minced fresh ginger

1 scallion, cut into 3-inch lengths and shredded

beef with tomato and onion

Since the 1940s, Chinese and Polynesian restaurants from California to Washington, D.C., have been serving beef with tomato and onion as an alternative to the chop suey and chow mein on their menus. Waiters would sometimes even bring the steaks on a sizzling platter with the tangy and sweet tomato and onion sauce still bubbling. Nowadays, you are more likely to get this dish on a diner plate or in a Styrofoam container, but with this recipe you can once again taste the beef piping hot, seconds from the wok.

serves 4 as part of a multicourse meal

1. Marinate the beef: In a medium bowl, stir together the soy sauce, rice wine, and cornstarch until the cornstarch is dissolved. Add the beef and stir gently to coat. Let stand at room temperature for 10 minutes.

2. Prepare the sauce: In a small bowl, stir together the Worcestershire sauce, soy sauce, and rice wine. Set aside.

3. Heat a wok over high heat until a bead of water sizzles and evaporates on contact. Add 1 tablespoon of the peanut oil and swirl to coat the bottom. Add the beef and stir-fry for about 2 minutes, until light brown on the outside but not yet cooked through. Scoop the beef from the wok and set aside.

4. Add the remaining 1 tablespoon oil to the wok and swirl to coat the bottom again. Add the onions and garlic and stir-fry until just fragrant, about 30 seconds. Add the tomatoes and cook for 1 to 2 minutes, breaking each up into 2 or 3 pieces with your spatula. Add the sauce and stir so that the vegetables are well coated. Return the beef to the wok and stir-fry for about another minute, until the beef is cooked through. Season with pepper to taste. Transfer to a plate and serve.

marinade

1 tablespoon soy sauce

1 tablespoon Chinese rice wine or dry sherry

1 teaspoon cornstarch

1 pound flank steak, cut against the grain into ¼-inch-thick slices

sauce

2 tablespoons Worcestershire sauce

1½ teaspoons soy sauce

1½ teaspoons Chinese rice wine or dry sherry

2 tablespoons peanut or vegetable oil

1 yellow onion, thickly sliced

2 garlic cloves, chopped

1 12-ounce can whole peeled tomatoes, drained

Freshly ground black pepper

sweet and sour pork

Sweet and sour are two of the five flavors of classical Chinese cooking (along with salty, pungent, and bitter), and *gu lo yuk,* as the dish is called, is a favorite way to prepare pork in Cantonese cooking. The recipe here has a lighter sauce more akin to the Cantonese version than the overly sweet goopiness of bad takeout versions, but it also has the crispy boneless pork that any lover of this dish will recognize. I prefer fresh pineapple, but if you like your dish sweeter, use canned pineapple and reserve some of the juice from the can to add to the sauce in place of fresh pineapple juice.

serves 4 as part of a multicourse meal

1. Prepare the batter: In a medium bowl, stir together the eggs, cornstarch, and flour. The batter should be liquidy enough to coat the pork. If the batter looks too dry, add 1 to 2 tablespoons of water and stir again. Add the pork and stir gently to coat. Let stand at room temperature for 10 minutes.

2. Prepare the sauce: In a small bowl, stir together the water, ketchup, pineapple juice, cider vinegar, Worcestershire sauce, soy sauce, and sugar until the sugar is dissolved. Set aside.

3. Heat the peanut oil in a wok until it registers 350°F on an instant-read oil thermometer. Working in 2 or 3 batches, add the first batch of pork cubes and fry until golden brown on the outside and cooked through, 4 to 5 minutes. Remove the pork with a slotted spoon and drain on a plate lined with paper towels. Remove any excess bits of batter from the oil with a slotted spoon or fine-mesh strainer. Continue frying the rest of the pork.

4. Transfer the oil to a heat-proof container. (It will take about 1 hour to fully cool, after which you can transfer it to a container with a tight lid to dispose of it.) Wipe up any food remains in the wok with paper towels, being careful not to touch the metal directly with your hands.

5. Heat the remaining 1 tablespoon oil in the wok or a skillet over medium-high heat. Add the garlic and ginger and stir-fry until just aromatic, about 20 seconds. Add the pineapple and the sauce and stir to coat the vegetables. Let the sauce simmer for

batter

2 large eggs, beaten

¼ cup cornstarch

¼ cup all-purpose flour

1 pound boneless pork loin, cut into
    1-inch pieces

sauce

3 tablespoons water

2 tablespoons ketchup

2 tablespoons fresh pineapple juice,
    or juice from the canned
    pineapple, or substitute orange
    juice

1½ tablespoons cider vinegar

1 tablespoon Worcestershire sauce

1 tablespoon soy sauce

2 tablespoons sugar

2 cups peanut or vegetable oil for
    frying, plus 1 tablespoon for
    stir-frying

1 tablespoon minced garlic

1 teaspoon minced fresh ginger

1 cup fresh or canned bite-size
    pineapple chunks

special equipment

Instant-read oil thermometer

2 to 3 minutes to allow the pineapple to become tender (about 1 minute for canned pineapple). Return the pork to the wok and toss until well coated with the sauce. Transfer to a plate and serve.

twice-cooked pork

I started making twice-cooked pork at home after trying it a few times in Sichuan restaurants and having serious cravings a day later. Called *hui guo rou* in Chinese, which translates to "meat returned to the wok," this extremely popular Sichuan dish is like bacon coated with a pleasantly musky bean and chili sauce. The "twice-cooked" part refers to the pork belly being first simmered in salted water until fully cooked, then sliced and stir-fried in its own juices. The pork is then cooked with a hearty sauce of fermented black beans, chili bean sauce, and fragrant rice wine. I like to use leeks as the only vegetable; minimalism on the plate allows the pork to be the star of the show. Twice-cooked pork is a little more time-consuming than some of the stir-fries featured in the book thus far, but worth a try if you want to truly understand why Sichuan food is so addictive.

serves 4 as part of a multicourse meal, or 2 as a main dish

1. Place the pork belly in a pot of salted water and bring to a boil. Lower the heat and simmer for about 40 minutes, skimming the water to remove any grayish foam on top, until the pork is cooked through. Drain and let cool. When the pork is cool enough to handle, pat completely dry with paper towels and slice into ¼-inch-thick pieces.

2. Rinse the black beans to remove any excess grit. Drain and lightly mash them with the back of a spoon.

3. Prepare the sauce: In a small bowl, mix together the soy sauce, rice wine, chili bean sauce, sesame oil, and sugar. Set aside.

4. Heat a wok or large skillet over high heat until a drop of water sizzles and evaporates on contact. Add the peanut oil and swirl to coat the bottom. Working in 2 batches, stir-fry the pork slices until golden brown on each side. Transfer the pork to a plate lined with paper towels. The pork belly will render extra fat, so drain all but 1 tablespoon of oil from the wok, then repeat the process with the second batch.

5. Reheat the wok and stir-fry the black beans, ginger, and leeks for 1 to 2 minutes, or until the leeks are softened. Return the pork to the wok. Pour in the sauce, stirring until everything is well combined. Transfer to a plate and serve.

1 pound pork belly

1 tablespoon fermented black beans, or substitute 1 tablespoon Chinese black bean paste

sauce

1 tablespoon soy sauce

1 tablespoon Chinese rice wine or dry sherry

1 tablespoon chili bean sauce

1 teaspoon sesame oil

1 teaspoon sugar

1 tablespoon peanut or vegetable oil

1 tablespoon minced fresh ginger

1 leek, white part only, thinly sliced

chinese barbecued pork

It takes a strong person to resist slices of glistening roast pork, crisp and dripping with caramelized juices. But when you get *char siu,* translated as Chinese "barbecued pork," at a Cantonese restaurant, the familiar red color will most likely be from a little food coloring. A small amount of dye isn't harmful, but sometimes a restaurant will go overboard, and you end up with barbecued pork that has a glowing magenta exterior. The solution is to make *char siu* at home. Rather than using food coloring, you can get a good reddish-brown color from dark soy sauce, a little hoisin sauce, and honey. Dark soy sauce is the best to use for adding more color and giving it a sweet, aged flavor, but you can always substitute regular soy sauce. The key is marinating the meat for 2 to 3 hours to allow the flavors to seep in before roasting the pork belly. You can serve roast pork as is, as part of a multicourse meal, or added to noodle soup with shiitakes and Chinese greens. Leftovers (if there are any!) can be used for Yangzhou Fried Rice (page 152), Roast Pork Lo Mein (page 144), or Singapore Noodles (page 146).

serves 4 to 6 as part of a multicourse meal

1. Marinate the pork belly: In a large bowl, mix together the rice wine, dark soy sauce, sugar, garlic, hoisin sauce, and five-spice powder. Rub the pork belly with the marinade mixture and marinate for 2 to 3 hours in the refrigerator.

2. Preheat the oven to 325°F.

3. Hold up the pork for a few seconds to allow excess marinade to drip off, then place the pork in a roasting pan. Brush the top with the honey. Roast the pork for about 45 minutes, flipping over the pork belly halfway through and brushing honey on the other side. The pork is done when the outside begins to crisp and blacken and the center of the pork belly strip feels firm.

4. Remove the pork from the oven and let it cool for 5 to 10 minutes. Transfer to a cutting board and cut into thin slices. Arrange the slices on a plate and serve.

marinade

2 tablespoons Chinese rice wine or dry sherry

2 tablespoons dark soy sauce, or substitute regular soy sauce

2 tablespoons sugar

2 garlic cloves, minced

1½ teaspoons hoisin sauce

½ teaspoon Chinese five-spice powder

1 pound whole pork belly, skin removed

2 tablespoons honey

the la choy dragon

At the start of Prohibition in 1920, when some Americans were creating illegal spirits in their bathtubs, two recent college graduates in Detroit began using their bathtubs for a more wholesome activity: growing bean sprouts. Wally Smith and Ilhan New began producing bean sprouts to sell at Smith's general store and soon discovered that canning their sprouts would extend their shelf life. Although neither of the men was Chinese, within four years they had launched a successful company with a full line of Chinese goods, including bean sprouts, bamboo shoots, chow mein noodles, and "Chinese sauce," as soy sauce was often called at the time. Their company, La Choy, grew to be one of America's largest producers of canned and prepackaged foods.

After decades of creating recipe books and print ads encouraging homemakers to cook Chinese food with their products, La Choy began searching for something new to appeal to TV audiences. In 1965 the company met with a young puppeteer named Jim Henson, whose character Rowlf the Dog regularly appeared on *The Jimmy Dean Show*. They asked if Henson could create a dragon that breathed real fire for a new televised ad campaign. The result, after months of design and pyrotechnics testing, was Delbert the La Choy Dragon. Clumsy but affable, Delbert stumbled his way through commercials, proclaiming the greatness of La Choy's chow mein and other products, while breathing fire at the canned foods. "La Choy chow mein. As crisp and good as the takeout kind," he would say, before letting out a burst of flame. "Because it's quick-cooked in dragon fire!"

The La Choy Dragon, voiced by Jim Henson himself, interacted with live human characters and taught them how easy it was to cook with La Choy. It was the era when convenience foods really took off, and the message was that even something as seemingly intimidating as preparing Chinese food was within the reach of any homemaker. The La Choy Dragon was the first full-size puppet Henson ever created, and later even became a model for *Sesame Street*'s Big Bird. The Muppets' fire-breathing mechanism did sometimes cause accidental fires on the set, but it was a small price to pay for pushing the boundaries of puppeteering . . . and Chinese food advertising.

cumin lamb stir-fry

Cumin is used in a lot of western Chinese cooking, but it periodically shows up in Hunan and Sichuan cooking as well. My favorite cumin stir-fries involve lamb, which has a great, lightly gamy essence that matches well with the strong flavors of cumin and chili. Boneless leg of lamb is as easy to stir-fry as beef and has the advantage of not having tough fibers, so you don't have to fret about which way the grain is going before slicing. To maximize the flavor and intoxicating aroma of this dish, I recommend toasting and grinding whole cumin instead of using preground cumin.

serves 4 as part of a multicourse meal

1. Marinate the lamb: In a medium bowl, stir together the soy sauce, rice wine, and cornstarch until the cornstarch is dissolved. Add the lamb and stir gently to coat. Let stand at room temperature for 15 minutes.

2. If you're using whole cumin seeds, toast the cumin seeds in a dry skillet over medium heat, shaking the pan occasionally, until fragrant, 1 to 2 minutes. Grind with a mortar and pestle or with a clean spice grinder.

3. Prepare the seasoning: In a small bowl, combine the cumin, sesame oil, Sichuan pepper, and black pepper. Set aside.

4. Heat a wok or large skillet over high heat until a bead of water sizzles and evaporates on contact. Add the peanut oil and swirl to coat the bottom. Add the lamb and allow it to cook undisturbed for 1 minute so that it begins to sear. Stir-fry for about another minute, or until the lamb browns on the outside but is not cooked through. Add the garlic, ginger, and leeks, and stir-fry for about 1 minute, until the leeks are wilted. Add the seasoning mixture, stirring so that the lamb is well coated. Stir-fry until the lamb is cooked through, another 1 to 2 minutes. Transfer to a plate and serve.

marinade

1 tablespoon soy sauce

1 tablespoon Chinese rice wine or dry sherry

2 teaspoons cornstarch

1 pound boneless leg of lamb, cut into ¼-inch-thick slices

seasoning

2 teaspoons whole cumin seeds, or substitute 3 teaspoons ground cumin

2 teaspoons sesame oil

½ teaspoon Sichuan pepper, or substitute crushed red pepper flakes

¼ teaspoon freshly ground black pepper

1 tablespoon peanut or vegetable oil

2 teaspoons minced garlic

1 teaspoon minced fresh ginger

1 leek, white part only, thinly sliced

moo shu pork

Originally from northern China, moo shu pork may have been the first non-Cantonese Chinese dish to become popular with American diners. It was also the first Chinese dinner entrée that you were encouraged to eat with your hands. Diners received a communal plate of stir-fried shredded pork and vegetables, such as shiitake mushrooms, carrots, and cabbage, to be scooped into a flour pancake and folded up. Vegetables and even protein varied from restaurant to restaurant (some served moo shu chicken or moo shu tofu), but the commonality was that all the ingredients had to be shredded. Sometimes restaurants even used tortillas in place of the slightly thinner moo shu pancakes, which may be why in Southern California this dish is sometimes still translated as "Chinese burritos." Despite the many different varieties of moo shu dishes, however, I still like to stick with the more traditional pork. You can pick up frozen moo shu wrappers (sometimes labeled Mandarin pancakes) at any big Chinese market. Wrappers will need to defrost according to package instructions before they are used. If you can't find actual moo shu pancakes, flour tortillas make a good substitute. This is a very flexible dish, welcoming to other shreddable ingredients that might strike your fancy. The only requirement comes at serving time—that your guests roll up their sleeves and dig in.

serves 4 as part of a multicourse meal

1. Marinate the pork: In a medium bowl, stir together the soy sauce, rice wine, and cornstarch until the cornstarch is dissolved. Add the pork and stir gently to coat. Let stand at room temperature for 20 minutes.

2. Prepare the sauce: In a small bowl, stir together the rice wine, dark soy sauce, hoisin sauce, sesame oil, and white pepper. Set aside.

3. Heat a wok or large skillet over high heat until a bead of water sizzles and evaporates on contact. Add 1 tablespoon of the peanut oil and swirl to coat the bottom. Add the pork and stir-fry until the outside is no longer pink, 2 to 3 minutes. Transfer the pork to a plate lined with paper towels and set aside.

4. Swirl the remaining 1 tablespoon oil in the wok. Add the garlic, ginger, and scallions and stir-fry until just aromatic, about 30 seconds. Add the shiitake mushrooms, cabbage, carrots, and bean sprouts and stir-fry for 1 to 2 minutes, or until the vegetables start to wilt.

marinade

1½ teaspoons soy sauce

1½ teaspoons Chinese rice wine or dry sherry

2 teaspoons cornstarch

1 pound boneless pork loin or pork chop, sliced into thin, bite-size strips

sauce

2 tablespoons Chinese rice wine or dry sherry

1 tablespoon dark soy sauce, or substitute regular soy sauce

1 tablespoon hoisin sauce

1 tablespoon sesame oil

¼ teaspoon ground white pepper

5.   Pour the sauce into the wok in a circular motion so that it drizzles down the sides of the wok and picks up the flavorings along the way. Return the pork to the wok and cook for another minute, stirring so that everything is well mixed. Transfer the pork and vegetables to a serving plate and serve with moo shu wrappers and a dish of extra hoisin sauce on the side.

6.   To eat, place a wrapper on your plate and spread 1 or 2 spoonfuls of pork and vegetables in the middle of the pancake. Spoon a dollop of hoisin sauce over the filling. Fold the bottom of the pancake up slightly, then fold in the 2 sides until you have 3 enclosed sides (like folding a burrito, with 1 side open). Hold the bottom or the sides as you start eating.

2 tablespoons peanut or vegetable oil

1 teaspoon minced garlic

1 teaspoon minced fresh ginger

2 scallions, chopped

6 fresh shiitake mushrooms, stems removed and caps thinly sliced

5 or 6 large napa cabbage leaves, cut into thin strips

1 medium carrot, julienned

1 cup fresh bean sprouts

12 moo shu wrappers, defrosted according to package instructions, or thin flour tortillas

Hoisin sauce for serving

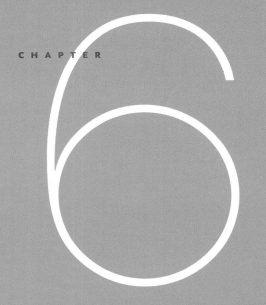

seafood

clams with black bean sauce

This classic Cantonese dish of stir-fried clams is a standard for any Chinatown restaurant that prides itself on its seafood. The fermented black beans, a favorite Chinese accompaniment for shellfish, add an intense, salty flavor, while the zing of fresh ginger balances out the earthy sauce. If you'd like to create a complete meal with other Cantonese favorites, try serving with Wonton Soup (page 55), Chinese Steamed Fish with Ginger and Scallions (page 106), and Chinese Broccoli with Oyster Sauce (page 125).

serves 4 as part of a multicourse meal

1. Rinse and scrub the clams under cold water, changing the water several times, to remove any grit. Discard any open clams that don't close when tapped. Drain the clams in a colander and gently wipe them dry with paper towels. (This will prevent hot oil from spitting when you add the clams to the wok.)

2. Rinse the black beans to remove any grit. In a small bowl, mash the black beans with the back of a spoon.

3. Heat a wok or large skillet over high heat until a bead of water sizzles and evaporates on contact. Add the peanut oil and swirl to coat the bottom. Add the black beans, chili sauce, garlic, and ginger and stir-fry until aromatic, about 30 seconds. Add the clams and stir-fry for another minute. Add the rice wine to release the brown bits from the bottom of the pan.

4. Pour in the chicken stock, cover, and allow the clams to steam for 5 to 6 minutes (4 to 5 minutes for Manila clams). Uncover the wok. The shells should now be fully open; discard any clams whose shells are still closed. Transfer the clams to a serving platter.

5. Allow the broth to simmer for another 1 to 2 minutes to reduce and thicken a bit more. Stir in the scallions before turning off the heat. Ladle the sauce over the clams and serve.

1½ pounds littleneck or Manila clams

2 tablespoons fermented black beans

1 tablespoon peanut or vegetable oil

1 teaspoon chili sauce

1 tablespoon minced garlic

1½ teaspoons minced fresh ginger

2 tablespoons Chinese rice wine or dry sherry

⅓ cup Chicken Stock (page 172)

1 scallion, thinly sliced

special equipment

Wok with lid

chinese steamed fish with ginger and scallions

for photo see page 102

When I teach Chinese cooking classes, I often have students who are intimidated by steaming fish in a wok. But once they've tried it, they're surprised by how easy it is. One of the most important steps is selecting the freshest fish. Go to a trusted seafood market to buy the fish; look for shiny, vibrantly colored flesh with no dry edges or pungent aromas. Back in your kitchen, you'll just need a wok with a lid, a plate or shallow pan that is smaller than the wok, and a wire steamer rack to elevate the plate (in a pinch, you can also use an inverted heat-proof bowl). As for the seasoning, just remember that less is more—the minimal flavorings coupled with the steaming really allow the natural flavor of the fish to shine through.

serves 4 as part of a multicourse meal

1. Prepare the sauce: In a small bowl, stir together the soy sauce, rice wine, sesame oil, and sugar until the sugar is dissolved.
2. Place the fillets in a heat-proof dish and pour the sauce over the fish. Scatter the ginger and half of the shredded scallions on top.
3. Fill the wok with 2 inches of water and bring to a boil. Carefully set the dish on the rack, then cover with the lid. Steam over high heat for 7 to 8 minutes; the flesh will be white when done. Carefully remove the dish from the wok with dry kitchen towels. Serve the fish as is, family style, or transfer to individual plates and spoon the juices from the dish over the fish. Garnish with the remaining scallions and serve.

sauce

2 tablespoons soy sauce

2 tablespoons Chinese rice wine or dry sherry

2 tablespoons sesame oil

½ teaspoon sugar

4 4-ounce white fish fillets, such as red snapper or sea bass, about 1 inch thick

1 1-inch piece fresh ginger, peeled and julienned

3 scallions, cut into 3-inch lengths and shredded

special equipment

Wire steamer rack or similar

Wok with lid

steamed mussels
with five-spice seasoning

Mussels are inexpensive and incredibly tasty, and cook quickly. After cleaning the mussels, the cooking time is less than 10 minutes and results in an impressive-looking dish that will no doubt wow your guests. The Chinese rice wine used for steaming complements the sweet brininess of the fresh shellfish. The other ingredients—Chinese five-spice powder, oyster sauce, shallots, and fresh ginger—combine to make a delicious, musky, and complex broth; be sure to have plenty of steamed rice on hand!

serves 4 as part of a multicourse meal

1. Rinse and scrub the mussels under cold water, changing the water several times, to remove any grit. Debeard the mussels by removing the stringy bits in the seam where the two shells meet. Discard any mussels with cracked shells or any with open shells that don't close when you gently tap them against the counter.

2. Prepare the sauce: In a small bowl, stir together the rice wine, oyster sauce, soy sauce, and five-spice powder. Set aside.

3. Heat a wok or large skillet over medium-high heat until a bead of water sizzles and evaporates on contact. Add the peanut oil and swirl to coat the bottom. Add the shallots, garlic, and ginger and stir-fry until aromatic, about 30 seconds. Add the sauce mixture. Carefully add the mussels and cover with a lid. Allow the mussels to steam for 4 to 5 minutes, then uncover. Discard any mussels that have not opened, then transfer the mussels to a serving dish.

4. Ladle the sauce over the mussels, then drizzle with the sesame oil. Sprinkle the chopped cilantro on top and serve.

2 pounds fresh mussels

sauce

½ cup Chinese rice wine or dry sherry

1 tablespoon oyster sauce

2 teaspoons soy sauce

1 teaspoon Chinese five-spice powder

1 tablespoon peanut or vegetable oil

2 shallots, finely chopped

2 teaspoons minced garlic

2 teaspoons julienned fresh ginger

1 tablespoon sesame oil

Small handful of fresh cilantro, chopped

special equipment

Wok with lid

sweet chili shrimp

This stir-fried shrimp dish is likely to be on the menu of your favorite Mandarin-style or Sichuan restaurant, maybe under the names Sichuan shrimp or chili shrimp. The sauce is tangy, sweet, and spicy with an edge of garlic; it may seem complex, but it actually requires few ingredients and less than 5 minutes of cooking time. And don't feel that you need to serve this with rice—though you may, with excellent results; the sauce is also sublime poured over al dente noodles.

serves 4 as part of a multicourse meal, or 2 to 3 as a main course

1. In a large bowl, toss the shrimp with the cornstarch, salt, and pepper.

2. Prepare the sauce: In a small bowl, stir together the soy sauce, honey, cider vinegar, and chili sauce. Set aside.

3. Heat a wok or large skillet over high heat until a bead of water sizzles and evaporates on contact. Add the peanut oil and swirl to coat the bottom. Add the garlic, ginger, and shallot and stir-fry until fragrant, 30 to 40 seconds. Toss in the shrimp and stir-fry about 2 minutes, until pink. Pour in the sauce and stir to coat the shrimp well. Transfer to a plate and serve.

1 pound large shrimp, peeled and deveined

2 teaspoons cornstarch

½ teaspoon salt

¼ teaspoon freshly ground black pepper

sauce

1 tablespoon soy sauce

1 tablespoon honey

1 tablespoon cider vinegar

1½ teaspoons chili sauce

1 tablespoon peanut or vegetable oil

2 teaspoons minced garlic

1 teaspoon minced fresh ginger

1 shallot, finely chopped

shrimp with lobster sauce

Shrimp with lobster sauce is a classic Cantonese-American favorite that's also a misnomer: The dish doesn't contain lobster at all. The name comes from the fact that the sauce—made with fermented black beans, ground pork, ginger, scallions, and eggs—is similar to the sauce Cantonese restaurants in Chinatown have used for preparing lobster since the 1940s and 1950s (see Lobster Cantonese, page 112). Many restaurants, particularly on the East Coast, serve a "white" lobster sauce that leaves out the fermented black beans. I prefer the original black bean version for its heady aroma and depth of flavor, but you can make the recipe below without the black beans. You'll want to serve this with a good portion of rice to soak up all the rich, velvety morsels.

serves 4 as part of a multicourse meal

1. Rinse the fermented black beans to remove any excess grit. In a small bowl, mash the beans with the back of a spoon.

2. Heat a wok or large skillet over high heat until a bead of water sizzles and evaporates on contact. Add 1 tablespoon of the peanut oil and swirl to coat the bottom. Add the shrimp and stir-fry for 1 to 2 minutes, or until the outsides begin to turn orange but the insides are not yet cooked through. Transfer the shrimp to a plate and set aside.

3. Swirl the remaining 1 tablespoon oil into the wok. Add the garlic, ginger, and mashed black beans and cook until just fragrant, about 30 seconds. Add the pork and stir-fry for about 2 minutes, breaking up the meat with a spatula, until the pork begins to lose its pink color. Pour in the chicken stock, rice wine, soy sauce, and oyster sauce and mix until well combined. Stir in the cornstarch mixture and bring the liquid to a simmer. Allow the sauce to simmer for about 1 minute, or until it becomes thick enough to coat the back of a spoon. Add the shrimp.

4. Drizzle in the beaten egg while stirring so that the egg strands spread in the sauce instead of clumping. Season to taste with pepper. Transfer to a deep plate, sprinkle on the scallions, and serve.

1 tablespoon fermented black beans

2 tablespoons peanut or vegetable oil

1 pound large shrimp, peeled, with tails left intact, and deveined

1 teaspoon minced garlic

1 teaspoon minced fresh ginger

½ pound ground pork

½ cup Chicken Stock (page 172)

2 tablespoons Chinese rice wine or dry sherry

1 tablespoon soy sauce

1 tablespoon oyster sauce

1 teaspoon cornstarch, dissolved in 1 tablespoon water

1 large egg, beaten

Freshly ground black pepper

1 scallion, green parts only, thinly sliced

takeout cartons

These nifty square containers weren't always used for hauling egg rolls and lo mein from a restaurant to your doorstep. Folded paper buckets were originally designed as a pail for freshly shucked oysters, back when oysters were abundant and sold cheaply from market stalls and street stands in New York. Coated with wax or plastic and theoretically leak-proof, the paper pails were also used to carry ice cream at one point. It wasn't until the years following World War II, when inexpensive Chinese food became more and more in demand, that Chinese restaurant owners realized the cartons were ideal for holding food their customers wanted to carry out.

n the 1970s, the Fold-Pak company came out with a printed design that has become a standard—a red pagoda on the side and red "Thank you" on top. The company now produces two-thirds of all the Chinese takeout containers sold in the United States every year, including microwaveable versions held together by glue instead of wire and environmentally friendly cartons made with recycled paper. But while the folded takeout carton is recognizable to any American as a vessel for carrying Chinese food, they are practically nonexistent in China, where Styrofoam containers, plastic tubs, and even plastic bags are standard.

lobster cantonese

Lobster Cantonese is one of those nostalgic dishes from yesteryear that you can still find at old-school Cantonese restaurants. The earthy sauce of black beans and pork coats the lobster beautifully, but is still light enough for the sweet, delicate flavor of the lobster to shine through. Though it may seem intimidating, the dish is actually quite easy to prepare, if you're able to have your fishmonger cut the lobster into pieces for you. Then it's all a matter of lining up the ingredients and stir-frying. If you're feeling brave and want to do the cutting yourself, see the note below, but have your fishmonger kill the whole lobster for you.

serves 4 as part of a multicourse meal

1. Rinse the fermented black beans to remove any grit. Drain and mash the beans lightly with the back of a spoon.

2. Heat a wok or deep 14-inch skillet over high heat. Add the peanut oil and swirl to coat the bottom. Add the scallions, garlic, ginger, and black beans and stir-fry briefly until just aromatic, about 30 to 40 seconds. Add the pork and cook until no longer pink, 2 to 3 minutes.

3. Pour in the chicken stock and rice wine and bring the liquid to a boil. Add the lobster pieces and reduce the heat to a simmer. Toss with a spatula so the lobster is well coated with the sauce. Cover and allow the lobster to steam for about 5 minutes, or until the lobster's shell is red and the meat is opaque.

4. Add the cornstarch mixture and stir until the sauce has thickened enough to coat the back of a spoon. Drizzle the sesame oil over the lobster. Make a well in the middle and pour the egg over the sauce in a thin, circular stream; the egg will cook immediately and look like white strands in the sauce. Toss the lobster once more to coat it with sauce, then transfer to a platter and serve.

NOTE: To cut a lobster into pieces, twist off the claws and tails and catch any juices with a bowl, then use a lobster cracker to crack the shell of the claws in half and the shell of the body in several places. With kitchen shears, cut the claws, tail, and body into 12 even pieces, making sure the meat stays intact within the shell.

2 tablespoons fermented black beans

1½ tablespoons peanut or vegetable oil

2 scallions, white parts only, thinly sliced

2 garlic cloves, minced

2 teaspoons julienned fresh ginger

¼ pound ground pork

1 cup Chicken Stock (page 172)

2 tablespoons Chinese rice wine or dry sherry

1½ pounds whole uncooked lobster, cut into 12 pieces, or 1½ pounds lobster tails in the shells, each tail cut into thirds (see Note)

1 tablespoon cornstarch, dissolved in 2 tablespoons water

1 teaspoon sesame oil

1 large egg, beaten

special equipment

Wok or deep 14-inch skillet with lid

salt and pepper squid

This popular fried dim sum dish gets a makeover as a quick stir-fry, but still retains the flavor base of salt, black pepper, and Sichuan pepper that has made these tasty morsels so popular at restaurants. If you're hankering to re-create a dim sum experience at home, try pairing this dish with Fried Pork and Shrimp Wontons (page 42), Chinese Broccoli with Oyster Sauce (page 125), and Mango Pudding (page 159). You can also substitute shrimp for the squid and stir-fry it for 2 to 3 minutes in step 3.

serves 4 as part of a multicourse meal

1. With a sharp knife or kitchen shears, slice the body of the squid into rings about ½ inch thick. Trim the tentacles into 2- or 3-inch lengths.

2. In a small bowl, stir together the salt, black pepper, and Sichuan pepper.

3. Heat a wok or large skillet over high heat until a bead of water sizzles and evaporates on contact. Add the peanut oil and swirl to coat the bottom. Add the squid and sear undisturbed for 30 seconds, then sprinkle in the salt-pepper mixture. Stir-fry for another minute, or until the edges begin to curl. (Squid cook very quickly, so don't leave them in the pan too long or they will develop a rubbery texture.) Remove from the heat and garnish with the cilantro. Serve as is or with chili sauce.

1 pound squid, cleaned
½ teaspoon salt
½ teaspoon freshly ground black pepper
¼ teaspoon Sichuan pepper
1 tablespoon peanut or vegetable oil
Small handful of fresh cilantro
Chili sauce for serving (optional)

garlic shrimp with broccoli

Here, using freshly chopped garlic is key for getting a flavorful but light sauce that is a natural fit for the broccoli and onion. The extra bit of honey highlights the delicate sweetness of the shrimp. A fried rice side, such as Yangzhou Fried Rice (page 152) or Rainbow Vegetable Fried Rice (page 153), would go great with this dish.

serves 4 as part of a multicourse meal

1. Prepare the sauce: In a small bowl, stir together the chicken stock, soy sauce, sesame oil, rice vinegar, and honey. Set aside.

2. Heat a wok or large skillet over high heat until a bead of water sizzles and evaporates on contact. Add 1 tablespoon of the peanut oil and swirl to coat the bottom. Add the shrimp and cook until the outside is pink but the inside is not yet cooked through, about 2 minutes. Transfer to a bowl and set aside.

3. In the same wok, swirl in the remaining 1 tablespoon oil. Stir-fry the garlic, ginger, and onions until fragrant and the onions are translucent, about 1 minute. Add the broccoli and stir-fry for about another minute, or until the edges of the broccoli begin to crisp. Pour in the sauce, cover with a lid, and allow the broccoli to steam for about 3 minutes, until tender-crisp.

4. Remove the lid and return the shrimp to the wok. Stir until well coated with sauce. Season with salt and pepper to taste and serve.

sauce
- ⅔ cup Chicken Stock (page 172)
- 2 tablespoons soy sauce
- 1 teaspoon sesame oil
- 1 teaspoon white rice vinegar
- 1 teaspoon honey

- 2 tablespoons peanut or vegetable oil
- 1 pound large shrimp, peeled and deveined
- 4 to 5 garlic cloves, minced
- 1 1-inch piece fresh ginger, minced or grated
- 1 medium yellow onion, chopped
- 3 cups broccoli florets
- Salt and freshly ground black pepper

special equipment
- Wok with lid

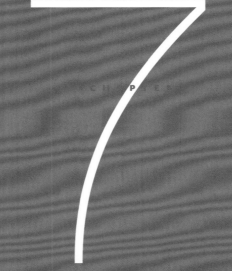

7

vegetables, tofu, & eggs

stir-fried sesame baby bok choy

Baby bok choy ranges in length from 3 to 5 inches. It's harvested young, and its tender texture makes it ideal for steaming, boiling, or stir-frying. Here, the finished dish has a nice nutty aroma from the sesame oil drizzled on at the end. Any number of stir-fries, including Kung Pao Chicken (page 65) and Sweet and Sour Pork (page 92), would benefit from having this simple vegetable dish on the side.

serves 4 as part of a multicourse meal

1. Trim and discard the rough bottoms from the baby bok choy. Separate the leaves, rinse, and pat dry.
2. In a small bowl, combine the soy sauce, rice wine, and sugar. Set aside.
3. Heat a wok or large skillet over medium-high heat until a bead of water sizzles and evaporates on contact. Add the peanut oil and swirl to coat the bottom and sides. Add the garlic and ginger and stir-fry until aromatic, 20 to 30 seconds. Add the bok choy and stir-fry for about 2 minutes, until crisp-tender. Add the soy sauce mixture and cook for another 30 seconds. Turn off the heat, and drizzle with sesame oil. Transfer to a serving plate and serve hot.

1 pound baby bok choy

sauce

1½ tablespoons soy sauce

1 tablespoon Chinese rice wine or dry sherry

½ teaspoon sugar

1 tablespoon peanut or vegetable oil

1 garlic clove, minced

1 1-inch piece fresh ginger, peeled and minced

2 teaspoons sesame oil

fresh versus dried shiitake mushrooms

Westerners cooking Chinese dishes that involve shiitake mushrooms sometimes face a dilemma of whether to used dried or fresh. When Chinese cooks make braises, dumplings, or soups, most of the time they will use dried mushrooms, favoring the dried type's more complex taste profile: The sun-drying process for shiitakes draws out the strong umami flavor. As Westerners, however, we've been taught that fresh ingredients (almost) always taste better than their dried equivalents. In addition, many people I've encountered, even adventurous eaters, may not like the slightly chewier texture of dried mushrooms.

Here is the general advice my mom passed down to me: In dishes where ingredients are few and the mushroom texture stands out, plump and juicy fresh shiitakes win out. However, in dishes that have more ingredients, such as Hot and Sour Soup (page 52) and Buddha's Delight (page 126), dried mushrooms lend a valuable umami flavor to the rest of the dish.

egg foo young with gravy

This classic egg foo young, filled with bean sprouts, ham, mushrooms, and scallions, will bring you back to the bygone days of neon Chop Suey signs and of strong rum cocktails with your Chinese dinner. Egg foo young doesn't have to be as oily or gloppy as some restaurant versions you may have eaten. Just a small amount of oil for every batch is enough for the eggs to get their signature crispy edges. The gravy, so delicious that you may end up pouring it all over your eggs, requires only four ingredients. Whether you're making egg foo young for breakfast, lunch, or dinner, it's easy to prepare and incredibly versatile. For variations on the filling, in place of the ham you can substitute shredded chicken, roast pork, cooked or raw shrimp, or cooked crab meat, or leave out meat and seafood altogether—the mushrooms provide a good amount of meaty flavor on their own.

serves 4 as part of a multicourse meal

1. Prepare the gravy: In a small saucepan, bring the chicken stock to a boil, then reduce the heat to a simmer. Stir in the soy sauce, hoisin sauce, and cornstarch mixture. Simmer for about another minute, until the sauce is thick enough to coat the back of a spoon. Reduce the heat to very low and cover the pot to keep the gravy warm.

2. Heat a wok or large skillet over medium-high heat until a bead of water sizzles and evaporates on contact. Add 1 tablespoon of the peanut oil and swirl to coat the bottom. Add the mushrooms, scallion whites, and bean sprouts and cook for 2 to 3 minutes, until the scallions are fragrant and the mushrooms and sprouts are slightly softened. Sprinkle in the ham so that it's evenly distributed. Stir in the soy sauce and sesame oil. Cook for another minute to allow the sauce to coat the vegetables and ham. Remove the vegetables and ham from the heat and set aside to cool for 2 to 3 minutes so that they won't cook the eggs when combined.

3. In a medium bowl, beat the eggs. Stir in the cooled vegetables and ham.

4. Heat the remaining 1 tablespoon oil in a large skillet over medium heat. Working in batches, ladle about ¼ cup of the mix-

gravy

¾ cup Chicken Stock (page 172)

1½ teaspoons soy sauce

1½ teaspoons hoisin sauce

1 tablespoon cornstarch, dissolved in 2 tablespoons water

2 tablespoons peanut or vegetable oil, plus more if necessary

3 or 4 fresh shiitake or cremini mushrooms, stems removed and caps thinly sliced

5 scallions, white and green parts separated, thinly sliced

1½ cups fresh bean sprouts

¼ cup chopped ham

1 tablespoon soy sauce

1 teaspoon sesame oil

6 large eggs

ture to form each pancake. Cook until golden brown, 1 to 2 minutes on each side, then transfer to a plate. Repeat with the remainder of the egg mixture, adding more peanut oil, if necessary.

5. Remove the sauce from the heat. Pour over the pancakes or transfer to a gravy boat to serve on the side. Garnish with the scallion greens and serve.

spicy garlic eggplant

Eggplant, with its meaty, mild flavor, is one of those vegetables that practically begs for strong, pungent spices and sauces. One Sichuan favorite is eggplant cooked with a hot chili-infused garlic sauce and studded with bits of pork. Use thin Asian eggplants for this dish; they are less bitter, more tender, and relatively seedless compared with Western eggplants. For the vinegar, Chinkiang black vinegar—an aged, smoky, and slightly sweet vinegar from China—is the best to use, but you can also substitute a good-quality balsamic vinegar.

serves 4 as part of a multicourse meal

1. Slice each eggplant lengthwise into quarters, then slice each quarter lengthwise again, forming 8 long strips. Cut each strip into bite-size pieces about 1 inch long.

2. Prepare the sauce: In a small bowl, mix together the chicken stock, soy sauce, black vinegar, chili oil, brown sugar, and Sichuan pepper. Set aside.

3. Heat a wok or large skillet over high heat until a bead of water sizzles and evaporates on contact. Add 1 tablespoon of the peanut oil and swirl to coat the bottom. Toss in the pork and stir-fry until crispy and starting to brown but not yet dry, 2 to 3 minutes.

4. Lower the heat to medium-high and swirl in the remaining 2 tablespoons oil. Carefully add the eggplant and stir-fry until the outsides become golden brown and the insides begin to soften, about 3 minutes. Add the scallions, garlic, and ginger and stir-fry until fragrant, about 30 seconds. Pour in the sauce and mix until well combined. Simmer for about 2 minutes to allow the eggplant to absorb the sauce. Transfer to a serving dish and serve hot.

1 pound (2 to 3) Asian eggplants

sauce

¼ cup Chicken Stock (page 172), or water plus a pinch of salt

1 tablespoon soy sauce

1 tablespoon Chinese black vinegar or good-quality balsamic vinegar

1 tablespoon chili oil

1 tablespoon light brown sugar

½ teaspoon ground Sichuan pepper, or substitute ¼ teaspoon crushed red pepper flakes

3 tablespoons peanut or vegetable oil

¼ pound ground pork

2 scallions, minced

2 garlic cloves, minced

1 tablespoon minced fresh ginger

mapo tofu

I almost always order mapo tofu at Sichuan restaurants, despite that voice in my head pushing me to try something new. The craving for this spicy, rustic tofu and pork dish is too hard to resist. Thinking about the mala ("numbing spiciness") flavor, the silky creaminess of the tofu contrasted with the slightly crispy pork, and the luscious, deep red sauce that wraps sublimely around steamed rice makes me surrender to the tried and true. The English translation of *mapo tofu*, "pockmarked mother's tofu," refers to an old woman in nineteenth-century Sichuan province who reportedly created the dish by cooking tofu in oil with plenty of dried chilies and Sichuan pepper. In Sichuan, the mapo tofu tends to be considerably spicier than elsewhere in China and in the United States. Feel free to adjust the amount of chili bean paste called for to give the dish more or less heat. For a vegetarian version that is no less satisfying, substitute ½ cup of chopped cremini or shiitake mushrooms for the ground pork.

serves 4 as part of a multicourse meal

1. Prepare the sauce: Rinse the black beans to remove any grit. In a small bowl, mash the black beans with the back of a spoon. Combine the black beans with the chicken stock, chili bean paste, rice wine, soy sauce, sesame oil, sugar, and Sichuan pepper. Set aside.

2. Heat a wok or large skillet over high heat until a bead of water sizzles and evaporates on contact. Add the peanut oil and swirl to coat the bottom. Add the pork and stir-fry until crispy and starting to brown but not yet dry, about 2 minutes, breaking up the pork with a spatula. Reduce the heat to medium, then add the leeks, garlic, and ginger and stir-fry until fragrant, about 1 minute.

3. Pour in the sauce and bring the liquid to a boil. Reduce the heat to a simmer. The liquid should now be a rich red color. Gently add the tofu cubes, being careful not to move them around too much or else they will break up. Allow the sauce to simmer for 2 to 3 minutes so that the tofu can cook and absorb the sauce.

4. Carefully push the tofu to the sides and create a small well in the middle of the wok. Stir the cornstarch mixture into the center. Allow the liquid to simmer for about another minute, until the sauce has thickened enough to coat the back of a spoon. Transfer to a deep plate or wide bowl, sprinkle the scallions on top, and serve hot.

sauce

- 1 tablespoon fermented black beans, or substitute black bean sauce
- 1 cup Chicken Stock (page 172)
- 2½ tablespoons chili bean paste
- 1 tablespoon Chinese rice wine or dry sherry
- 2 teaspoons soy sauce
- 2 teaspoons sesame oil
- 2 teaspoons sugar
- ½ teaspoon ground Sichuan pepper

- 2 tablespoons peanut or vegetable oil
- ½ pound ground pork or beef
- 2 leeks, white parts only, thinly sliced at an angle
- 2 garlic cloves, minced
- 1 teaspoon minced fresh ginger
- 1 pound (about 1 block) soft or medium-firm tofu, drained and cut into 1-inch cubes
- 1 tablespoon cornstarch, dissolved in 2 tablespoons water
- 1 scallion, green part only, thinly sliced

chinese broccoli with oyster sauce

Legend has it that oyster sauce, the viscous, caramel-colored staple essential to Cantonese cooking, was created completely by accident. In the late 1880s in the southern Chinese province of Guangdong, a restaurant owner named Lee Kum Sheung reportedly left a pot of oyster soup on the fire too long, returning to it only to find that his soup had reduced to a thick, dark brown liquid. He tasted it, found it incredibly flavorful, and later decided to mass-produce it under the brand Lee Kum Kee. In the 1930s, the company started selling oyster sauce in the United States. These days oyster sauce is typically made of oyster essence or oyster extract, though vegetarian versions use mushrooms as a base for a similar flavor. The thick pungent sauce became inseparable from Chinese takeout itself, finding its way into dishes such as Moo Goo Gai Pan (page 74) and Beef with Broccoli (page 87). It's also indispensable for one of the best vegetable sides in Chinatown restaurants: Chinese broccoli with oyster sauce. Called *gai lan* in Cantonese, Chinese broccoli has thick, flat leaves with small white buds, and has a slightly earthier taste than Western broccoli. This dish is so simple that it doesn't even need stir-frying; just simmer the sauce ingredients, briefly cook the broccoli, and drizzle the thickened sauce on top.

serves 4 as part of a multicourse meal

1. Prepare the sauce: In a small saucepan, stir together the oyster sauce, soy sauce, rice wine, sesame oil, garlic, ginger, and sugar. Bring the mixture to a boil, then reduce the heat to medium-low. Simmer for 1 to 2 minutes, stirring occasionally, to allow the garlic and ginger flavors to infuse. Turn off the heat and cover with a lid so that the sauce stays warm.

2. Bring a medium pot of water, enough to submerge the broccoli, to a boil. Add the broccoli and boil for about 3 minutes, until the stalks turn a darker green. The texture should be tender enough to easily pierce with a fork but still crisp. Drain well and transfer to a plate. Drizzle the sauce over the top and serve.

sauce

3 tablespoons oyster sauce

1 tablespoon soy sauce

1 tablespoon Chinese rice wine or dry sherry

½ teaspoon sesame oil

1 garlic clove, minced

1 teaspoon julienned fresh ginger

1 teaspoon sugar

1 pound Chinese broccoli, hard ends trimmed

buddha's delight

Buddha's Delight is traditionally served on the first day of Chinese New Year, a practice stemming from an old Buddhist custom of spiritual cleansing. In fact, the recipe's Cantonese name is simply *jai,* meaning "vegetarian food." Some ingredients, such as lily buds and bean thread noodles, may require a special trip to a Chinese market.

serves 4 as part of a multicourse meal

1. Soak the shiitake mushrooms and lily buds in a bowl of warm water for 15 to 20 minutes. Squeeze out the excess water. Discard the stems from the mushrooms and thinly slice the mushroom caps. (For extra mushroom flavor, reserve the soaking liquid and add it to the dish.) Slice the rough black ends off the lily buds and discard, cut the lily buds in half, and pull apart the strands.

2. Rinse the bamboo shoots and thinly slice them. Trim and discard the hard ends from the snow peas and cut the snow peas lengthwise. Drain and finely chop the water chestnuts.

3. In a large bowl, soak the bean thread noodles in enough warm water to cover for 10 minutes to soften them. Drain, shake off the excess water, and set aside.

4. Drain and rinse the tofu, then pat dry with paper towels. Slice the tofu into 1-inch cubes.

5. Prepare the sauce: In a small bowl, stir together the vegetable broth, soy sauce, hoisin sauce, sesame oil, and brown sugar. Set aside.

6. Heat a wok, Dutch oven, or deep 14-inch skillet over medium heat until a bead of water sizzles and evaporates on contact. Add the peanut oil and swirl to coat the bottom. Add the ginger and cook until fragrant, about 30 seconds. Add the mushrooms, lily buds, bamboo shoots, snow peas, water chestnuts, cabbage, and tofu. Add the sauce and the mushroom soaking liquid (if using) and bring to a boil. Reduce the heat to a simmer, cover, and cook for 3 to 4 minutes. Remove the lid, add the drained bean thread noodles, re-cover the wok, and simmer for about another 5 minutes, or until the noodles are cooked. (Don't worry if the dish looks a little soupy; the noodles will absorb the remaining broth.) Ladle everything into a deep serving dish and serve hot.

8 dried shiitake mushrooms

8 dried lily buds

¼ cup bamboo shoots (fresh or canned)

½ cup snow peas

¼ cup canned water chestnuts

4 ounces bean thread noodles

½ pound extra-firm tofu

sauce

2 cups Vegetable Broth (page 173)

3 tablespoons soy sauce

1½ tablespoons hoisin sauce

1 tablespoon sesame oil

1 tablespoon light brown sugar

1 tablespoon peanut or vegetable oil

1½ teaspoons minced fresh ginger

1 cup shredded napa cabbage

special equipment

Wok with lid, Dutch oven, or a deep 14-inch skillet

simple broccoli stir-fry

An order of your favorite chicken, beef, or pork dish from your local takeout often comes on a bed of Western broccoli. It's by no means traditional, but is nevertheless a vegetable we associate with comforting Chinese takeout. While you can certainly steam broccoli in your vegetable steamer or rice cooker, try this simple and flavorful stir-fry that takes no more effort than steaming.

serves 4 as part of a multicourse meal

1. Heat a wok or large skillet over medium-high heat until a bead of water sizzles and evaporates on contact. Add the peanut oil and swirl to coat the bottom. Add the garlic and stir-fry until fragrant, for about 20 seconds. Add the broccoli and stir-fry for about 1 minute, or until the outsides begin to crisp. Add the water, then immediately cover the wok with a lid. Allow the broccoli to steam, covered, for about 3 minutes, or until the water evaporates.

2. Remove the cover and salt and pepper to taste. Transfer to a plate and serve.

1 tablespoon peanut or vegetable oil
1 garlic clove, minced
4 to 5 cups broccoli florets
⅓ cup water
Salt and freshly ground black pepper

special equipment
Wok with lid

dry-fried green beans

In contrast to either snappy haricot verts or microwaved diner-style beans, Sichuan green beans are blistered and well cooked without being bland or mushy. With Sichuan pepper and dried chilies adding spice and smokiness to the flavor profile, these crisp yet tender beans become positively addictive. The most important thing to remember after washing your green beans is to dry them thoroughly before cooking; excess water droplets will make your hot oil spit. The trick to frying these green beans so that they are cooked through but not completely charred is using a bit more oil than you would for a stir-fry and briskly stirring the beans with a spatula. The 5 or 6 minutes of shallow frying allow the green beans to develop not only the characteristic wrinkled and blistery surface, but also a deep, caramelized flavor.

serves 4 as part of a multicourse meal

1. Rinse the green beans and dry them thoroughly; even a small amount of water will cause oil in the wok to spit. Cut the beans into 2-inch lengths.

2. Prepare the sauce: In a small bowl, stir together the rice wine, chili bean sauce, sesame oil, sugar, and salt until the sugar is dissolved. Set aside.

3. Heat a wok or large skillet over high heat until a bead of water sizzles and evaporates on contact. Add the peanut oil and swirl to coat the bottom. Add the green beans and stir-fry, keeping the beans constantly moving, for 5 to 6 minutes, or until the outsides begin to blister and the beans are wilted. Turn off the heat, remove the green beans, and set aside to drain on a plate lined with paper towels.

3. Remove all but 1 tablespoon of oil and reheat the wok. Add the chilies, Sichuan pepper, garlic, ginger, and scallions and stir-fry until fragrant, about 30 seconds. Add the mushrooms and stir-fry for about another minute, until the mushrooms have browned and started to crisp. Add the sauce. Return the green beans to the wok and stir-fry for about another minute. Transfer to a plate and serve hot.

¾ pound green beans

sauce

1½ teaspoons Chinese rice wine or dry sherry

1½ teaspoons chili bean sauce

½ teaspoon sesame oil

1 teaspoon sugar

½ teaspoon salt, plus more to taste

¼ cup peanut or vegetable oil

5 or 6 dried red chilies

¼ teaspoon ground Sichuan pepper

1 tablespoon minced garlic

1 teaspoon minced or grated fresh ginger

3 scallions, white parts only, thinly sliced

4 ounces fresh shiitake or cremini mushrooms, finely chopped

stir-fried water spinach with garlic

Few children love vegetables, but even as a toddler I loved these long stalks of water spinach that stayed crunchy even when wilted. Of course, it helped that my parents never called it spinach. The Chinese for water spinach is *kong xin cai,* which literally means "empty-hearted vegetable." Indeed, the hollow stalks have the advantage of holding on to all flavorings they are cooked with, and the leaves also sop up sauce very well. My favorite method of preparing water spinach is to simply stir-fry it with garlic and flavor it with a little oyster sauce and fish sauce, which the greens will eagerly soak up. Water spinach, with its long stalks and narrow, pointed leaves, is sold in Asian markets in very large bunches. While the bunch will look enormous, it actually cooks down a lot in the wok. To use, trim the thicker bottom halves of the stems, then cut the remaining top half of the stems and the leaves into 3-inch lengths. If you can't find Chinese spinach, you can substitute watercress or regular spinach; the latter takes 1 to 2 minutes less time to stir-fry.

serves 4 as part of a multicourse meal

1. Remove the hard end of the water spinach, about 2 inches up the stems. Cut the remainder, the thin stems and leaves, into 3-inch lengths. Rinse the water spinach and drain, shaking out as much water as possible.

2. Heat a wok or large skillet over high heat until a bead of water sizzles and evaporates on contact. Add the peanut oil and swirl to coat the bottom. Add the garlic and stir-fry until the outsides begin to brown, 20 to 30 seconds. Add the water spinach and stir occasionally as the large bunch wilts and shrinks, 2 to 3 minutes.

3. Add the oyster sauce, fish sauce, and red pepper flakes (if using). Stir so that the seasonings are well mixed in. Allow the water spinach to cook about another minute, or until it is fully wilted but still vibrant green. (The sauce will be somewhat liquidy.) Transfer to a plate and serve.

1 to 1½ pounds fresh water spinach

1 tablespoon peanut or vegetable oil

5 garlic cloves, smashed

1 tablespoon oyster sauce

1 tablespoon fish sauce

½ teaspoon crushed red pepper flakes (optional)

stir-fried asparagus tips

Chinese menus often list this dish as "stir-fried asparagus tips" because the cooks cut the vegetable into easy-to-handle pieces. But in reality you can use the asparagus whole minus the thick, woody end. Although asparagus will often be served in an entrée with chicken or beef, cooking it alone highlights the crisp-tender texture.

serves 4 as part of a multicourse meal

1. Prepare the sauce: In a small bowl, stir together the vegetable broth, soy sauce, sesame oil, and sugar until the sugar dissolves. Set aside.

2. Heat a wok or large skillet over medium-high heat until a bead of water sizzles and evaporates on contact. Add the peanut oil and swirl to coat the bottom. Add the garlic and briefly stir-fry until aromatic, about 20 seconds. Add the asparagus and bamboo shoots and stir-fry for another 2 minutes. Stir in the sauce and allow it to simmer for another minute. Add salt to taste. Transfer to a plate, sprinkle sesame seeds on top, and serve.

sauce

1 tablespoon Vegetable Broth (page 173) or water

1 tablespoon soy sauce

½ teaspoon sesame oil

½ teaspoon sugar

1 tablespoon peanut or vegetable oil

1 garlic clove, minced

1 pound asparagus, thick woody ends trimmed off and remaining stalks cut into 2-inch segments

¼ cup canned sliced bamboo shoots, drained

Salt

½ teaspoon white sesame seeds

marbled tea eggs

Every once in a while, if you're lucky, you may run across a dim sum restaurant, Chinese bakery, or Taiwanese teahouse that serves tea eggs. Tea eggs may be sold alone, or top off a noodle dish, or come as a side with an order of pork chops, but the common denominator is that they smell and taste too good to pass up. The aromas of tea, cinnamon, and soy sauce are intoxicating, and the flavors seep through the lightly cracked eggshells to give the eggs a nice earthiness. Getting the marbling effect at home is as simple as cracking the egg once it's cooked. You can use any black tea, but avoid green tea, which is too astringent to use for tea eggs. The eggs can be simmered for 1 to 2 hours; longer simmering means a more intense flavor and color. Once the eggs are cooked, you can eat them hot or cold as a snack. I've made lazy meals out of just two eggs over ramen and oyster sauce, or chopped up eggs over fried rice. You can even serve them as dressed-up appetizers at a party, cut in half with a dollop of caviar on top.

makes 6 to 8 eggs

1. Add enough water to a medium pot to cover the eggs. Bring the water to a boil and cook for about 10 minutes, or until the eggs are hard-boiled.

2. Remove the eggs with a strainer and run under cold water until they are cool enough to handle. Tap the eggs with the back of a butter knife to crack them evenly all around, being careful not to peel off the shells. Return the eggs to the pot.

3. In the same pot, add the tea bags, soy sauce, brown sugar, star anise, cinnamon, black peppercorns (if using), and orange peel (if using). Add enough water to cover the eggs by an inch. Bring the liquid to a boil, then lower the heat to a bare simmer. Allow the eggs to simmer for 1 to 2 hours, longer for a more intense flavor and color.

4. Remove from the heat and drain the eggs, saving a little of the liquid to serve with the eggs if you choose. You can either peel and serve the eggs immediately or store them in the fridge for up to 4 days in a tightly covered container. Serve as a snack or as an addition to rice or noodles.

6 to 8 eggs, any size

2 tea bags black tea

½ cup soy sauce

1 tablespoon light brown sugar

2 pieces star anise

1 cinnamon stick

1 teaspoon cracked black peppercorns (optional)

2 to 3 strips dried orange peel (optional)

8

noodles & rice

dan dan noodles

I have eaten many four-alarm Sichuan meals and I've actually come to miss and crave the *mala* sensation (numbing spiciness) of spicy Dan Dan Noodles if I don't eat Sichuan for a week or more. Sichuan pepper is worth seeking out to add spiciness, but you can substitute crushed red pepper flakes. I've adjusted the recipe to tone down the heat for newcomers to Sichuan food who may be wary of having a scorched tongue. But don't worry, chili fans; you can just double or triple the amount of chili oil for the true Sichuan experience.

serves 4 as part of a multicourse meal, or 2 to 3 as a main course

1. Bring a large pot of water to a boil and cook the noodles according to the package instructions. Drain the noodles, rinse under cold water, and drain again thoroughly. Transfer the noodles to a serving dish.

2. Prepare the sauce: In a medium bowl, whisk together the soy sauce, rice wine, sesame paste, black vinegar, chili oil, sesame oil, sugar, Sichuan pepper, and water. Pour half the sauce over the noodles and toss to evenly distribute the sauce. Set aside. Reserve the other half of the sauce for the pork.

3. Heat a wok or large skillet over medium-high heat until a bead of water sizzles and evaporates on contact. Add the peanut oil and swirl to coat the bottom. Add the garlic, ginger, and scallion whites and cook until fragrant, about 30 seconds. Add the pork and stir-fry until it is a little crispy on the outside and no longer pink, 3 to 4 minutes. Stir in the reserved sauce and cook for another minute. Salt to taste.

4. Spoon the cooked pork mixture over the noodles, sprinkle the scallion greens and peanuts on top, and serve.

> The name "dan dan noodles" refers to the way noodles were once sold back in Sichuan province. Noodle peddlers would hoist street poles, called "dan dan," across their shoulders to balance baskets of noodles and fiery sauce as they walked through town.

12 ounces thin dried Chinese egg or wheat noodles

sauce

2 tablespoons soy sauce

2 tablespoons Chinese rice wine or dry sherry

1½ teaspoons Chinese sesame paste or tahini

1 tablespoon Chinese black vinegar, or substitute good-quality balsamic vinegar

3 tablespoons chili oil (adjust according to your tolerance of spiciness)

2 teaspoons sesame oil

1 teaspoon sugar

½ teaspoon ground Sichuan pepper, or substitute ¼ teaspoon crushed red pepper flakes

¼ cup water

1 tablespoon peanut or vegetable oil

2 teaspoons minced garlic

1 teaspoon minced fresh ginger

2 scallions, white and green parts separated, thinly sliced

½ pound ground pork or beef

Salt to taste

Handful of dry-roasted peanuts, finely chopped

beef chow fun

Beef chow fun is one of the best-loved noodle dishes in Cantonese cuisine, served at both high-end restaurants and hole-in-the-wall spots. Unlike many other Chinese noodle dishes, it incorporates the technique of dry stir-frying, which means that no stocks or sauces are used other than a small amount of soy sauce and oyster sauce. In this dish, the beef and noodles develop a lightly caramelized flavor from the pan searing. Bigger Chinatowns usually have specialty noodle and tofu shops that make wide rice noodles fresh every day. It's best to use them the same day you buy them. If you can't find fresh wide rice noodles, use dried wide rice noodles and follow the soaking instructions on the packaging.

serves 4 as part of a multicourse meal, or 2 to 3 as a main course

1. Marinate the beef: In a medium bowl, stir together the rice wine, soy sauce, and cornstarch until the cornstarch is dissolved. Add the flank steak and stir gently to coat. Allow the beef to marinate at room temperature while you prepare the other ingredients.

2. Prepare the seasoning: In a small bowl, stir together the the rice wine, oyster sauce, sesame oil, and sugar until the sugar is dissolved. Set aside.

3. In a small bowl, rinse the fermented black beans with water to remove any grit. Mash them with the back of a spoon.

4. If your fresh noodles are still in a sheet and not precut, slice them into ½-inch-wide strips. If you're using dried noodles, soak them according to the package instructions.

5. Heat a wok or large skillet over high heat until a bead of water sizzles and evaporates on contact. Add 1 tablespoon of the peanut oil and swirl to coat the bottom. Add the garlic and ginger and stir-fry until just fragrant, about 20 seconds. Add the beef and allow it to sear on one side undisturbed for about 1 minute. Add the black beans. Stir-fry for about another minute until the beef is brown on the outside but not yet cooked through. Transfer everything to a plate and set aside. Wipe out any stray bits of garlic or black beans in the wok with a paper towel.

marinade

1 tablespoon Chinese rice wine or dry sherry

1 tablespoon soy sauce

1 teaspoon cornstarch

½ pound flank steak, cut against the grain into ¼-inch-thick slices

seasoning

3 tablespoons Chinese rice wine or dry sherry

2 tablespoons oyster sauce

2 teaspoons sesame oil

1 teaspoon sugar

1 tablespoon fermented black beans

1 pound wide fresh rice noodles or 12 ounces wide dried rice noodles

3 tablespoons peanut or vegetable oil

2 teaspoons minced garlic

2 teaspoons minced fresh ginger

3 scallions, julienned

6.   Add the remaining 2 tablespoons oil and swirl to coat the bottom again. Spread the noodles in the wok in one layer and allow to cook over high heat undisturbed for 1 minute, until the edges of the noodles begin to crisp. Add the scallions and bean sprouts and stir-fry for about another minute, until they begin to wilt. Return the beef to the wok and pour in the seasoning mixture. Stir-fry for about 1 minute, making sure the beef and noodles are evenly coated with seasoning. Add pepper to taste. Transfer to a plate and serve.

4 ounces (about 2 cups) fresh bean sprouts
Freshly ground black pepper

chicken chow mein

Americans have been enjoying chow mein since Chinese restaurants first opened in the United States more than a century ago. Not only was this dish of scrumptious noodles served in Chinese restaurants, but within a few decades lunch counters at department stores such as Woolworth's and New York delis such as the famed Reuben's were dishing it out to urbanites on the go. Today, chow mein has slowly disappeared from the menus of non-Chinese eateries, but it remains a trusty standby at almost every Chinese restaurant. The name *chow mein* simply means "stir-fried noodles," which still opens the dish to wide interpretation. Hong Kong–style Cantonese restaurants stir-fry the noodles with enough oil to render them potato chip–crunchy, while at the other end of the spectrum, some restaurants barely stir-fry the noodles at all. I like to stir-fry the noodles alone in the wok, so they pick up some browning but are still soft enough to soak up the lip-smacking sauce. This recipe calls for chicken, but you can substitute thinly sliced beef, pork, or shrimp.

serves 4 as part of a multicourse meal

1. Soak the shiitake mushrooms in warm water for 15 to 20 minutes. Squeeze out the excess water. Discard the stems and thinly slice the mushroom caps.

2. Bring a large pot of water to a boil and cook the noodles 1 to 2 minutes less than stated in the package instructions, or just before al dente. Drain the noodles, rinse under cold water, and drain again thoroughly. Transfer to a bowl and toss with the sesame oil.

3. In a small bowl, stir together the soy sauce and rice wine. Add the chicken, toss to coat, and let stand at room temperature for 10 to 15 minutes.

4. Prepare the sauce: In a small bowl, stir together the chicken stock, soy sauce, hoisin sauce, and pepper. Set aside.

5. Heat a wok or large skillet over high heat until a bead of water sizzles and evaporates on contact. Add 1 tablespoon of the peanut oil and swirl to coat the bottom. Add the chicken and stir-fry until no longer pink on the outside but not yet cooked through, about 2 minutes. Add the onions, bell peppers, carrots, bean sprouts, and mushrooms. Cook for another 2 minutes, until the vegetables are tender-crisp and the chicken is cooked through. Remove from the wok and set aside.

6 dried shiitake mushrooms

10 ounces thin dried Chinese egg noodles

2 teaspoons sesame oil

marinade

1 tablespoon soy sauce

½ tablespoon Chinese rice wine or dry sherry

½ pound boneless, skinless chicken breasts, cut into ¼-inch-thick slices

sauce

¼ cup Chicken Stock (page 172)

1½ tablespoons soy sauce

1 tablespoon hoisin sauce

¼ teaspoon freshly ground white or black pepper

continued

6. Swirl the remaining 2 tablespoons oil into the pan. When the oil is hot and glistening, add the noodles and stir-fry until some of the strands turn golden, about 2 minutes. Make a well in the middle of the noodles and pour in the sauce. Return the chicken and vegetables to the wok and stir until everything is well coated and heated through. Transfer to a plate and serve.

3 tablespoons peanut or vegetable oil

1 medium onion or ½ large onion, thinly sliced

½ green bell pepper, sliced into thin strips

1 medium carrot, julienned

1 cup fresh bean sprouts

the chow mein sandwich

Since the 1930s, the residents of Fall River, Massachusetts, have been chowing down on the chow mein sandwich, a local favorite that has become a regular item even on school cafeteria menus. As the story goes, the sandwiches—hamburger or hot dog buns stuffed with crispy noodles, meat, and vegetables, all doused with brown gravy—took off during the Depression because it was cheaper than a full portion of chow mein yet just as filling. Families, packs of students, and workers from the textile mills alike would congregate at the Chinese restaurants, where you could get a hefty sandwich plus full-scale restaurant service, all for the price of a nickel.

The popularity of the sandwich spread as far as Rhode Island and Brooklyn's Coney Island, where it was served at the original Nathan's Famous for decades. Fall River's Oriental Chow Mein Company, a tiny family-owned operation that's also one of the world's largest suppliers of chow mein noodles, even offers a chow mein mix for preparing sandwiches at home. Today, in the twenty-first century, the cheap and hefty sandwich is still beloved in its hometown and surrounding communities as not only a delicious portable meal and vestige of Depression-era frugality, but also a fond memory of childhood.

taiwanese beef noodle soup

Taiwanese beef noodle soup, while delicious year-round, is one of those dishes that I crave when cold weather arrives. The soup has an incredibly complex, smoky, and spicy flavor that's perfect for beating the winter doldrums. The beef is first seared, then cooked in an aromatic broth flavored with star anise, garlic, ginger, and chili bean sauce. It's important to simmer the pot at a low temperature, with the broth barely bubbling, so that the beef can get a melt-in-your-mouth tenderness. The dish freezes well, so you can divide up any leftovers into small batches to freeze and reheat as desired.

serves 4 to 6 as a main course

1. Pat the beef chuck dry and slice it into large cubes 1½ to 2 inches thick. Sprinkle with salt.

2. Heat a wok, Dutch oven, or large pot over medium-high heat until a bead of water sizzles and evaporates on contact. Add the peanut oil and swirl to coat the bottom. Add the beef and sear until golden brown, about 3 minutes. Add the garlic, ginger, and chili bean sauce and cook for about 20 seconds to release the aromas. Add the rice wine to release any flavorings from the bottom.

3. Add enough water to cover the beef by 1 inch and the soy sauce, brown sugar, star anise, and crushed red pepper flakes. Bring the liquid to a boil. Reduce the heat to a gentle simmer and skim off any foam that rises to the top. Cover and continue to cook at a gentle simmer for about 2 hours, or until the beef is fork-tender, replenishing the water if it reduces too much to cover the beef.

4. Transfer the beef to a cutting board. Holding each piece at the end with a fork, cut the beef cubes into ½-inch-thick slices. Strain the beef broth into another pot and discard the solids. Bring the broth to a boil. Toss in the bok choy and cook in the broth for about 3 minutes, or until the bok choy is crisp-tender.

5. Meanwhile, bring another pot of water to a boil and cook the noodles according to the package instructions. Drain well.

6. Divide the noodles, beef slices, and vegetables into serving bowls and ladle the beef broth over. Serve hot.

2 pounds beef shank or beef chuck, preferably bone-in

Salt

2 tablespoons peanut or vegetable oil

2 garlic cloves, smashed

2 1-inch pieces fresh ginger

2 tablespoons chili bean sauce

¼ cup Chinese rice wine or dry sherry

½ cup soy sauce

2 tablespoons light brown sugar

2 whole star anise

¼ teaspoon crushed red pepper flakes

1 pound baby bok choy, hard end discarded and leaves separated

1 pound thin dried Chinese egg noodles or wheat noodles

roast pork lo mein

Lo mein is a noodle dish that often is confused with chow mein, and many Chinese restaurants further the confusion by using the two names interchangeably. The dishes are similar, both featuring noodles mixed with stir-fried meat and vegetables and a savory sauce. But whereas chow mein refers to parboiled and stir-fried noodles, lo mein refers to noodles that are fully cooked separately and quickly tossed with sauce in the wok. The roast pork in this recipe is char siu, the same gorgeous reddish-brown pork often displayed and sold in Chinatown shop windows. Instead of buying the pork ready-made, you can also roast your own at home (see Chinese Barbecued Pork, page 97). For the egg noodles, you can use any that are thin and round; spaghetti will also work.

serves 4 as part of a multicourse meal

1.   Bring a medium pot of water to a boil. Add the noodles and cook according to the package instructions until al dente, or the minimum amount of time suggested by the package. Drain the noodles, rinse under cold water, and drain again, shaking well to remove excess water. Return the noodles to the pot, toss with the sesame oil until the noodles are well coated, and set aside.

2.   Prepare the sauce: In a small bowl, combine the soy sauce, oyster sauce, rice wine, and honey. Set aside.

3.   Heat a wok or large skillet over high heat until a bead of water sizzles and evaporates on contact. Add the peanut oil and swirl to coat the bottom. Add the garlic, ginger, and scallions and stir-fry until aromatic, about 30 seconds. Add the mushrooms and cook until softened, 1 to 2 minutes.

4.   Add the noodles and pork. Pour in the sauce mixture and toss with tongs or chopsticks until the noodles and pork are heated through and well coated with sauce. Transfer to a platter and serve.

12 ounces, thin dried Chinese egg noodles

2 tablespoons sesame oil

sauce

3 tablespoons soy sauce

1½ tablespoons oyster sauce

1½ tablespoons Chinese rice wine or dry sherry

1½ teaspoons honey

1 tablespoon peanut or vegetable oil

1½ teaspoons minced garlic

1 teaspoon minced or grated fresh ginger

3 scallions, cut into 2-inch lengths

4 or 5 fresh shiitake mushrooms, thinly sliced

½ pound Chinese Barbecued Pork, store-bought or homemade (page 97), cut into small, bite-sized pieces

singapore noodles

These stir-fried rice vermicelli noodles, coated with curry powder and chili paste and tossed with juicy Chinese Barbecued Pork (page 97) and plump shrimp, make an ideal quick one-plate lunch. The version that we get in American Chinatowns actually originated in Hong Kong, where enterprising chefs most likely concocted the noodle dish as a spicy alternative to the milder Cantonese dishes on their menus, christening it Singapore Noodles based on the heavier use of curry in Singaporean and Malaysian cooking. Rice noodles are extremely absorbent, so they will soak up all the liquid flavorings during stir-frying and pack some heat in each bite. I strongly recommend using a large wok for this, because the volume of ingredients is too much for even a 14-inch skillet, and the thin rice noodles tend to stick to stainless steel.

serves 4 as part of a multicourse meal

1. In a large bowl, soak the rice noodles with enough warm water to cover, for about 10 minutes. Drain and shake off the excess water. With kitchen shears, cut the noodles into 4- to 5-inch lengths and set aside.

2. Prepare the sauce: In a small bowl, stir together the chicken stock, rice wine, soy sauce, sugar, salt, and pepper. Set aside.

3. Heat a wok over high heat until a bead of water sizzles and evaporates on contact. Add 1 tablespoon of the peanut oil and swirl to coat the bottom and sides. Add the shrimp and stir-fry for about 2 minutes, until pink on both sides but not yet cooked through. Transfer the shrimp to a plate and set aside.

4. Swirl the remaining 2 tablespoons oil into the wok. Add the garlic and ginger and stir-fry until just aromatic, about 20 seconds. Add the onions, bell peppers, and bean sprouts and stir-fry for about 2 minutes, until the vegetables are slightly softened. Add the curry powder and chili paste and stir-fry for about another 30 seconds, until the curry is fragrant. Pour in the chicken sauce and bring the liquid to a simmer.

5. Add the noodles and cook, stirring often, for 2 to 3 minutes, until most of the liquid has been absorbed. Return the cooked shrimp to the wok and add the roast pork and scallions. Cook for another 1 to 2 minutes, until the pork is heated through. Transfer to a plate and serve.

10 ounces thin dried rice vermicelli

sauce

¾ cup Chicken Stock (page 172)

2 tablespoons Chinese rice wine or dry sherry

1 tablespoon soy sauce

½ teaspoon sugar

½ teaspoon salt

¼ teaspoon freshly ground black pepper

3 tablespoons peanut or vegetable oil

½ pound large shrimp, peeled and deveined

1 tablespoon minced garlic

1 tablespoon minced fresh ginger

½ yellow onion, thinly sliced

1 red bell pepper, thinly sliced

1 cup fresh bean sprouts, rinsed and drained

1½ tablespoons Madras curry powder

2 teaspoons chili paste

½ pound Cantonese roast pork, store bought or homemade (Chinese Barbecued Pork, page 97), cut into matchsticks

3 scallions, cut into 2-inch lengths

chop suey

Forget about the gloppy versions of chop suey you may have seen in restaurants. Though it has a reputation for being an outmoded faux-Chinese dish, chop suey actually draws from a long tradition of Chinese mothers stir-frying odds and ends they had left over. This basic recipe is far from being bland and overly starchy, and it is so good your guests just may ask for seconds. Think of the recipe as more of a guide than a strict list to follow. The spirit of chop suey is using up leftovers, so feel free to substitute any type of leftover protein for the chicken, including beef, pork, sausage, deli meats, seafood, tofu, or hard-boiled eggs. You can also easily substitute vegetables that you already have in your fridge, including celery, lettuce, peas, and green beans. Just be sure to chop everything up into bite-size pieces. If you have leftover gravy or pan juice from a roast, I encourage you to substitute that for the oyster sauce. You can serve this over leftover rice.

serves 4 as a main course

1. If the leftover chicken is in large pieces, chop it up into small, bite-size pieces.

2. Heat a wok or 14-inch skillet over medium-high heat until a bead of water sizzles and evaporates on contact. Add the peanut oil and swirl to coat the bottom. Add the onions and stir-fry for about 1 minute, or until it is aromatic. Add the mushrooms, bell peppers, cabbage, and bean sprouts and and stir-fry for 2 to 3 minutes.

3. Pour in the chicken stock. Stir in the soy sauce, rice wine, and oyster sauce. Season to taste with salt and pepper. Make a well in the center of the wok by pushing the vegetables and meat to the side, then stir the cornstarch mixture into the sauce in the well. Allow the sauce to simmer for about another minute, or until the sauce is thick enough to coat the back of a spoon. Either mix the rice into the chop suey before serving or serve the chop suey over rice.

2 cups leftover cooked chicken, or substitute another leftover cooked protein

1 tablespoon peanut or vegetable oil

1 medium onion, chopped

6 to 8 fresh shiitake or cremini mushrooms, chopped

1 large bell pepper, chopped

2 cups shredded cabbage

1 cup fresh bean sprouts

⅓ cup Chicken Stock (page 172) or Vegetable Stock (page 173)

1 tablespoon soy sauce

1 tablespoon Chinese rice wine or dry sherry

1 tablespoon oyster sauce

Salt and freshly ground black pepper

1½ teaspoons cornstarch, dissolved in 2 tablespoons water

3 to 4 cups leftover plain rice, fried rice, or instant rice

chop suey: how it all began

It's impossible to tell the story of Chinese food in America without detailing the history of Chop Suey, a stir-fried mishmash of meat and vegetables drenched in a brown sauce. Mysterious in origins and humble in appearance, chop suey somehow captured the hearts and taste buds of Americans for more than a century before it started to fade in popularity. Just what is Chop Suey, and where in the world did it come from?

One theory of Chop Suey's origin is that a group of hungry Caucasian laborers stumbled into a San Francisco Chinatown restaurant late one evening and demanded to be served. The cook, low on ingredients, improvised and served a stir-fried plate of leftovers, calling it a name that sounded like chop suey. Another theory is that the dish was introduced to Americans during the 1884 visit of Chinese diplomat Li Hong Zhang, who, according to newspaper accounts, tucked into his favorite dish of Chop Suey at a grand banquet at the Waldorf Astoria. A more likely scenario, however, is that chop suey came out of the meals of Chinese railroad workers in the nineteenth century, who needed to feed themselves with whatever meat and vegetables they could find. *Jup sui,* literally translated as "odds and ends," is simply what the Cantonese call a dish of recooked leftovers. It's highly probable that over time, *jup sui* became anglicized as Chop Suey. As Chinese restaurants grew in number and chop suey became more popular, the cooking became more standardized to include uniform cuts of meat in a brown gravy with vegetables such as bean sprouts, bamboo shoots, and mushrooms.

Chop Suey, seen as exotic fare, became increasingly popular in the early 1900s, venturing beyond Chinese restaurants. It was served at department store lunch counters and trendy Manhattan nightclubs. Chop Suey was also inspiration for musicians and artists. As least two Jazz Age songs, Louis Armstrong's "Cornet Chop Suey" and Sidney Bechet's "Who'll Chop Your Suey When I'm Gone?" became popular with the flapper set in the 1920s. Edward Hopper's 1929 painting *Chop Suey* depicts fashionable diners in an elegant Chinese restaurant, having tea at their tables, while a CHOP SUEY sign hangs outside the window.

Over time, the popularity of chop suey waned as American diners discovered more and more regional cuisines with unique flavors, including Sichuan, Hunan, and Shanghainese. It is still possible, however, to find Chinese restaurants across the United States that serve Chop Suey, and customers who still hunger for it after all these years.

pineapple fried rice

The secret to making delicious fried rice is stir-frying with cold leftover rice. Rice that has been cooled is firmer and has less moisture, and it develops the signature crispy texture more easily in the wok. Just remember to break up your rice into smaller clumps before stir-frying. This delicious fried rice, typical of the offerings at American Cantonese restaurants, pairs chopped ham with the sweet taste of the tropics.

serves 4 as part of a multicourse meal, or 2 as a main course

1. Break up the cold cooked rice into smaller clumps.
2. Heat a wok or large skillet over medium-high heat until a bead of water sizzles and evaporates on contact. Add the peanut oil and swirl to coat the bottom. Add the shallots and bell peppers and stir-fry until fragrant and the edges of the shallots begin to crisp, about 1 minute. Move the shallots and bell peppers to the side, creating a well in the middle. Toss in the rice and break up any remaining clumps with a spatula.
3. Stir in the oyster sauce, soy sauce, and rice wine. Continue to stir-fry until the rice starts to turn golden, about 2 minutes. Add the pineapple and ham. Give everything in the wok a few quick stirs so that the ham and pineapple are heated through. Transfer to a large bowl or plate and serve hot.

3 cups leftover cooked white rice

2 tablespoons peanut or vegetable oil

2 shallots, finely chopped

½ red bell pepper, finely chopped

1 tablespoon oyster sauce

1 tablespoon soy sauce

1 tablespoon Chinese rice wine or dry sherry

1 cup fresh pineapple, cut into ½-inch bite-size cubes

¼ cup chopped thickly sliced ham

yangzhou fried rice

for photograph see page 134

This classic fried rice is another favorite menu item at Chinese restaurants, maybe because the pairing of roast pork and plump pieces of shrimp is so irresistible. Named for the city of Yangzhou in China, the dish did not actually originate there, but was christened by a government official who once worked for the city. The authentic version of Yangzhou fried rice uses leftover Chinese Barbecued Pork (page 97), which gives the dish its distinct sweet flavor. But if you don't have any on hand, chopped-up honey ham makes a fine substitute.

serves 4 as part of a multicourse meal

1. Break up the cold cooked rice into smaller clumps.
2. Heat a wok or large skillet over medium-high heat until a bead of water sizzles and evaporates on contact. Add 1 tablespoon of the peanut oil and swirl to coat the bottom. Add the egg, spread it as thinly as possible, and cook undisturbed for 2 minutes, until cooked through. Transfer to a cutting board and chop into bite-size pieces.
3. Add another 1 tablespoon of the peanut oil and swirl to coat the bottom and sides. Add the shrimp and stir-fry for 1 to 2 minutes, or until cooked through. Transfer to a plate and set aside.
4. Swirl in the remaining 1 tablespoon oil. Add the scallions and stir-fry briefly until aromatic, about 20 seconds. Stir in the rice, breaking apart any remaining clumps with a spatula. Add the roast pork, peas, and chopped egg. Stir-fry for another 2 to 3 minutes, until the rice starts to turn golden and the peas have thawed. Return the shrimp to the wok. Season to taste with salt and pepper. Transfer to a large plate or bowl and serve hot.

3 cups leftover cooked white rice

3 tablespoons peanut or vegetable oil

1 large egg, whisked

¼ pound shrimp, peeled, deveined, and diced

1 scallion, thinly sliced

¼ pound leftover Chinese Barbecued Pork (page 97), or substitute honey ham, diced

1 cup frozen peas

Salt and freshly ground black pepper

rainbow vegetable fried rice

The beauty of vegetarian versions of fried rice is that they can be as colorful as your supermarket's produce section or local farmers' market allows. I like to use peas, purple cabbage, and red and yellow bell peppers to go with blackish shiitake mushrooms. Remember to break up your leftover rice into smaller clumps before it goes into the wok, so that it fries up and develops a crispy texture more easily.

serves 4 as part of a multicourse meal

1. Break up the cold cooked rice into smaller clumps.
2. Heat a wok or large skillet over medium-high heat until a bead of water sizzles and evaporates on contact. Add the peanut oil and swirl to coat the bottom and sides. Add the scallions and garlic and stir-fry until just fragrant, about 20 seconds. Add the mushrooms, peas, red and yellow bell peppers, and cabbage and stir-fry for another 1 to 2 minutes.
3. Stir in the rice, breaking up any remaining clumps with a spatula. Drizzle the soy sauce and sesame oil over the rice. Continue cooking the rice, stirring constantly, until the rice starts to turn golden and is well mixed with the vegetables, 2 to 3 minutes. Transfer to a large bowl or plate and serve hot.

3 cups leftover cooked white rice

2 tablespoons peanut or vegetable oil

1 scallion, finely chopped

1 garlic clove, finely chopped

4 or 5 fresh shiitake, cremini, or white button mushrooms, finely chopped

¼ cup frozen peas

1 large red bell pepper, diced

1 large yellow bell pepper, diced

1 or 2 large purple cabbage leaves, chopped

2 tablespoons soy sauce

1 teaspoon sesame oil

chicken congee

Congee is the chicken noodle soup of Asia, the homey one-pot dish used to nurse a common cold, hangovers, or a hungry stomach. Most countries in Asia have their distinct versions of this rice porridge, but China may have the upper hand with regard to variety of ingredients, throwing in anything from lettuce and carrots to preserved salted duck eggs and shredded dried pork. Chicken is a favorite meat to use for congee because you can make the chicken broth base at the same time. It takes about an hour for the rice to break down, giving the finished congee a creamy texture. If you have leftover rice, you can cut the cooking time in half.

serves 4 to 6 as a main course

1. Put the chicken in a large pot with the water and bring to a boil, skimming the foam on top as needed.

2. Rinse the rice and add it to the pot. (Don't worry about the large amount of liquid compared with the small amount of rice; the liquid will reduce and the rice will puff up during the hour of cooking.) Stir in the ginger, scallion whites, and rice wine. Reduce to a low simmer and cook, uncovered, for about 30 minutes.

3. Remove the cooked chicken from the pot and allow it to cool while you continue to cook the congee at a low simmer. When the chicken has cooled enough to handle, shred the meat and return it to the pot, discarding the bones. Continue to cook until the congee reaches the consistency of loose oatmeal, 20 to 30 minutes more, stirring occasionally so that the rice doesn't get stuck to the bottom of the pot. Salt and pepper to taste. Drizzle the sesame oil on top. Transfer to individual bowls, top with the scallion greens and peanuts, and serve.

NOTE: You can also make chicken congee in a slow cooker instead of a pot on the stove. Program the slow cooker for the fastest setting (about 4 hours). A half hour before the congee is done, remove and shred the chicken and return it to the congee to reheat for the remaining time.

1 pound skinless bone-in chicken thighs or legs

6 to 8 cups water

1 cup uncooked long-grain rice, or substitute 3 cups cooked rice

1 3-inch piece fresh ginger, peeled and cut into 2 or 3 pieces

2 scallions, white and green parts separated, thinly sliced

2 tablespoons Chinese rice wine or dry sherry

Salt and ground white pepper to taste

2 teaspoons sesame oil

½ cup roasted salted peanuts, chopped

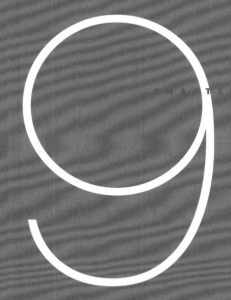

sweets

mango pudding

Many desserts that originate from Hong Kong have a curious commonality: They involve a fair amount of seemingly old-fashioned canned products. Mango pudding became popular in Hong Kong in the 1950s and 1960s, when the island territory's agricultural industry was just starting up and canned evaporated milk was the main stable dairy source. (In later years, as Hong Kong rapidly modernized, canned products went from necessities to nostalgic cultural mainstays. Even today, with such a wide variety of homegrown food and rare imported products available, Hong Kongers still love their Spam, Horlicks, and Ovaltine.) In the past few decades, Mango Pudding has become a fixture in the United States as well, in both dim sum restaurants and Chinatown dessert shops. At home, Mango Pudding is incredibly easy to make using a blender or food processor. Be sure to use ripe mangoes, as they will be sweeter and juicier. The hardest part might just be waiting for the dessert to chill before digging in.

serves 4 to 6

1. Peel the mangoes and slice the flesh from the pit. Put the slices into a blender or food processor and puree until smooth.

2. In a large glass bowl, add the hot water to the gelatin and stir until dissolved. Let the gelatin mixture stand for about 3 minutes. Add the evaporated milk and sugar and stir until the sugar is completely dissolved. Add the mango puree and mix well.

3. Pour the mixture into ramekins, wineglasses, or small shallow dishes. Cover with plastic wrap and chill in the refrigerator for at least 2 hours, or overnight. After the pudding is chilled, garnish with mango slices, raspberries, or kiwi slices (if using).

2 large ripe mangoes (makes about 2 cups mango puree)

½ cup hot water

1 envelope unflavored gelatin

½ cup evaporated milk

¼ cup sugar

Fresh mango slices, raspberries, or kiwi slices for garnish (optional)

special equipment

Blender or food processor

almond cookies

In 1972 noted chef and food writer James Beard wrote in his classic tome *American Cookery* that Chinese almond cookies "have been favorites in homes or bakeries on the West Coast for almost a hundred years, and their fame has spread." Indeed, in the post–World War II era, restaurants such as Cathay House in Boston, Don the Beachcomber in Palm Springs, and Tommy Wong's in Los Angeles would serve almond cookies on the dessert menu, alongside fortune cookies and "litchi" nuts. Over time, almond cookies have become more of a Chinese bakery treat, but their nutty fragrance and lightly sweet crunch are no less inviting. This recipe is an easy way to whip up dozens of these cookie classics, whether or not you live close to a Chinatown bakery.

makes about 3 dozen cookies

1. Preheat the oven to 325°F.
2. In a standing electric mixer fitted with the paddle attachment, combine the flour, sugar, baking soda, and salt. Beat in the softened butter a few pieces at a time at low speed, until the texture resembles that of cornmeal. Beat in the eggs and almond extract until a smooth dough is formed.
3. Roll the dough between your palms into 1¼-inch balls and place them 2 inches apart on ungreased baking sheets. Using the palm of your hand, gently flatten each ball and place an almond in the middle of each. Brush the top of each cookie with egg glaze.
4. Bake for 18 to 20 minutes, or until the cookies are golden on top, rotating the top and bottom baking sheets halfway through. Transfer the cookies to a cooling rack and allow them to cool for at least 5 minutes before serving. The cookies will keep for up to 3 to 4 days in an airtight container.

2½ cups all-purpose flour

1 cup sugar

½ teaspoon baking soda

½ teaspoon salt

½ pound (2 sticks) unsalted butter, cut into pieces and softened

2 large eggs, beaten

2 teaspoons almond extract

40 whole almonds

1 large egg, beaten, for glaze

special equipment

Mixer with paddle attachment

chinese butter cookies

Around the Chinese New Year, Chinatown bakeries fill up with tins of butter cookies, waiting to be given as gifts to relatives. Of course, they're still sold and eaten year-round, and once you have just one of these bite-size cookies, it's hard to stop. They're a tad less sweet than American cookies, but their rich butteriness makes them irresistible.

makes about 40 small cookies

1. Preheat the oven to 375°F. Line a baking sheet with parchment paper.
2. In a standing electric mixer, cream the butter until smooth. Add the confectioners' sugar and cream until fluffy. Add the egg and vanilla extract. Slowly sift in the self-rising flour and beat until a smooth dough forms.
3. Add the dough to a cookie press and attach a star or flower-shape disk. Press the cookies onto the lined baking sheet, leaving 1 inch of space around each cookie.
4. Bake for 15 minutes, or until lightly golden on top. Transfer to a wire rack to cool completely before storing. The cookies can be stored at room temperature in an airtight container for 3 to 4 days.

12 tablespoons (1½ sticks) unsalted butter, softened
¾ cup confectioners' sugar
1 large egg
½ teaspoon pure vanilla extract
1½ cups self-rising flour

special equipment
Mixer with paddle attachment
Cookie press

coconut buns (cocktail buns)

Walk into a Chinatown bakery and chances are you'll see a handful of elderly patrons, chatting away with friends or lingering over coffee, Mini Egg Tarts (page 167), or something called a cocktail bun. Also known as Coconut Buns, these pillowy, golden buns with buttery coconut filling were created in the 1950s in Hong Kong, supposedly by bakers who wanted a way to use up extra bread and shredded coconut. *Gai mei,* literally "cock tail" in the animal sense, was just Cantonese slang for leftovers.

makes 10 to 12 buns

1. Dissolve the yeast in the very warm water. To proof the yeast, add the 2 teaspoons sugar and let stand for about 10 minutes. The yeast is ready when it has bubbled and the volume has at least tripled.

2. In a large bowl, mix together the remaining ⅓ cup sugar, the flour, and salt. Add the milk, butter, eggs, and proofed yeast and mix until well combined. Dust a clean work surface with flour and knead the mixture for about 5 minutes, until it forms a smooth, elastic dough. Add more flour if the dough seems too sticky.

3. Lightly grease a large bowl with canola oil. Place the dough in the bowl and cover with a clean kitchen towel or plastic wrap. Set the bowl in a warm place (such as near a radiator in the winter or inside a turned-off oven that has a pilot light) and let the dough rise for 1½ to 2 hours, or until it doubles in size. While the dough is rising, make the coconut filling.

4. In a small bowl, mix together the coconut flakes, sugar, and butter until the mixture has a pastelike consistency.

5. When the dough has doubled in size, punch it down and divide it in half. Divide each half into rounds the size of a tennis ball. Working one by one, flatten each ball with the palm of your hand, and use a rolling pin to roll each disk into a 5-inch circle. Place 1 heaping tablespoon of coconut filling in the center. Bring the sides up to encase the filling, pinching and sealing up the dough. Make sure the edges are well sealed to prevent the coconut filling from spilling out during baking.

dough

2 packets instant dry yeast

½ cup very warm water

⅓ cup sugar, plus 2 teaspoons for proofing the yeast

4 cups all-purpose flour

1 teaspoon salt

¼ cup whole milk

8 tablespoons (1 stick) unsalted butter, melted

2 large eggs

Canola or vegetable oil

coconut filling

1¼ cups finely shredded coconut flakes

¼ cup sugar

8 tablespoons (1 stick) unsalted butter, melted

topping

1 large egg

White sesame seeds

6. Place the buns, seam side down, 1 to 2 inches apart on a greased baking sheet. Let the buns rise on the baking sheet, uncovered, for another 10 to 15 minutes. The buns may rise up and the seams run into each other during baking, which is perfectly fine and how they are baked at Chinese bakeries.

7. Preheat the oven to 350°F.

8. To make an egg wash, whisk the egg in a small bowl. Lightly brush the tops of the buns with the egg wash and sprinkle with the sesame seeds.

9. Bake for 15 to 20 minutes, or until golden brown. Remove from the oven and let cool on a wire rack for at least 5 minutes before serving. The coconut buns will keep at room temperature in an airtight container for up to a week.

continued

NOTE: If you live in an arid climate or it's an otherwise dry day, start with 3½ cups flour and add more if the dough seems too sticky to knead.

fortune cookies, the curious origins

The fortune cookie, the crunchy and lightly sweet ending to every takeout meal, is such a symbol of American Chinese cuisine that it's hard to believe that they originated neither in China nor in the United States.

In *The Fortune Cookie Chronicles: Adventures in the World of Chinese Food,* author Jennifer B. Lee traces the origin of fortune cookies to nineteenth-century Japan, where cookies called *tsujiura senbei* (fortune crackers) filled with poetic paper messages were served alongside tea. They were brought to the United States by Japanese immigrants, who settled mainly around San Francisco and Los Angeles and opened bakeries. But just how did the fortune cookie become so closely linked to Chinese food instead? Japanese cuisine was virtually unknown to American diners in the early 1900s, so Japanese immigrants opened chop suey houses to earn a living, some serving fortune cookies to customers. Chinese-owned Chinese restaurants did the same. Some speculate that when Japanese-Americans were sent to internment camps during World War II and had to close down their bakeries, the Chinese set up fortune cookie shops to keep up with the demand for the cookies, whose popularity by that time had become pretty widespread.

For many years, fortune cookies were made by hand, with workers folding the hot, freshly baked cookies with bare fingers and using chopsticks to stuff the messages inside. Then in 1964, the first automated fortune cookie machine with mechanical fingers for folding was invented in San Francisco. Now a handful of companies in the United States produce around 3 billion cookies a year to sell in the United States and around the world. But despite the best efforts of one Beijing-based company, fortune cookies still haven't caught on in China, where customers are perplexed both by how to open the cookies and why you would put paper fortunes inside cookies in the first place.

mini egg tarts

for photograph see page 156

Egg tarts, the Chinese equivalent of the English custard tart, come from Hong Kong, where pastry chefs supposedly created these tarts so that their bakeries could compete with dim sum restaurants for customers at breakfast. These sugary golden treats are available in almost any American Chinatown, and some bakeries even have a cult following: At Golden Gate Bakery in San Francisco, weekend lines to buy their egg tarts, still warm from the oven, sometimes stretch down the block. But there's no need to live near a Chinatown to enjoy warm, flaky egg tarts—you can make similar oven-fresh egg tarts by following this recipe, which uses frozen piecrust to cut down on preparation time.

makes 12 to 15 mini egg tarts

1. Defrost the piecrust according to the package instructions. Roll out the crust onto a lightly floured surface. Use a rolling pin to roll out the dough so that it doubles in surface area and is about 1/8 inch thick. Use a cookie cutter or tall drinking glass that is 1½ inches wider than the muffin pan cups to cut the dough into rounds. Press the rounds firmly into the pan, pulling the dough up the sides of the muffin cups, being careful not to overstretch.

2. Preheat the oven to 350°F.

3. Stir together the heavy cream and milk. Stir in the caster sugar and cornstarch until everything is dissolved.

4. In a separate bowl, whisk the egg yolks. Add the yolks to the heavy cream mixture and stir until well incorporated. Strain the mixture into another bowl to remove any remaining solids. Stir in the vanilla extract.

5. Carefully fill the muffin cups about three quarters of the way with egg mixture. Bake in the oven for 20 to 25 minutes, until the custard is cooked through. Test the doneness by inserting a toothpick into the center; the custard is set if the toothpick can stand up on its own.

6. Remove the tarts from the oven and let them cool for 5 minutes. Remove the tarts from the muffin pan and transfer them to a wire rack to cool for another 5 to 10 minutes. Serve warm or at room temperature. The egg tarts will keep at room temperature in an airtight container for up to 3 days.

1 frozen rolled piecrust

All-purpose flour, for dusting

¼ cup heavy cream

¼ cup whole milk

½ cup caster sugar, or substitute granulated sugar finely ground in a food processor or coffee grinder

1½ teaspoons cornstarch

2 large egg yolks

½ teaspoon pure vanilla extract

special equipment

1 mini muffin pan

black sesame ice cream

In Hong Kong and mainland China, black sesame is as common an ice cream flavor as vanilla or chocolate is in the United States. After all, long before ice cream became popular in Asia, black sesame was a favorite ingredient for sweets, such as in the sesame balls served at dim sum, and black sesame dessert soup. One of the best versions of black sesame ice cream I've ever had this side of the Pacific is at the Chinatown Ice Cream Factory in New York's Chinatown. It is lightly speckled with ground black sesame, richly creamy, yet light and airy at the same time. The version that follows uses a light Philadelphia-style eggless base infused with the toasted black sesame and a hint of vanilla. The black sesame has an incredibly complex, nutty fragrance and flavor, almost like dark chocolate or French roast coffee. In fact, it pairs well with either, or topped with raspberries or strawberries, or simply by itself. The ice cream stores well in the freezer for up to a week, if the leftovers last that long.

makes 1 quart

1. Combine 1 cup of the heavy cream, the sugar, and salt in a medium pot over medium-low heat. Stir until the sugar is fully dissolved.
2. Pour the cream mixture into a bowl. Stir in the remaining 1 cup heavy cream, the milk, and vanilla extract. Cover the mixture and chill in the fridge for at least 3 hours or overnight.
3. When the mixture has chilled, grind the sesame seeds in a clean spice grinder. Pour the mixture into your ice cream maker, slowly pour in the ground black sesame, and churn according to the manufacturer's instructions. Transfer the ice cream to a freezer-safe container and freeze for at least 4 hours or overnight.

2 cups heavy cream

¾ **cup sugar**

⅛ **teaspoon salt**

2 cups whole milk

½ **teaspoon pure vanilla extract**

¼ **cup black sesame seeds**

special equipment

Ice cream maker

Spice grinder

10

the basics

chicken stock

Chicken stock forms the basis of many Chinese recipes, from soups to stir-fries. The best and most basic recipe requires only three ingredients other than water: chicken, ginger, and a tiny bit of salt. You can use a whole chicken or individual bone-in cuts. Store-bought chicken broth is lacking in flavor, but is acceptable in a pinch. Look for organic or free-range store-bought chicken broth, which tends to be lower in preservatives.

makes about 3 quarts (12 cups)

1. Trim as much skin and fat as possible from the chicken.
2. Fill a large pot with the water and add the chicken and ginger. Bring the liquid to a boil, then quickly lower the heat to a gentle simmer. Stir in the salt. Allow the stock to simmer, covered, for 2 hours, skimming the surface periodically and discarding the foam.
3. After about 2 hours, strain the chicken stock through a fine-mesh strainer into another pot or a large bowl and discard the solids. Allow the stock to cool to room temperature. Transfer to an airtight storage container and refrigerate for up to 4 to 5 days or freeze in small portions for future use. The chicken stock will keep up to 2 months in the freezer.

2 pounds cut-up whole chicken or bone-in chicken parts, such as legs and wings

3½ quarts water

2 1-inch-long pieces fresh ginger, peeled and thickly sliced

1 teaspoon salt

If you're trying to stretch a dollar, bone-in chicken thighs are a great value that serve dual purposes. Because they're in lower demand at the supermarket—due to the mistaken idea that thighs have a high fat content—they're often half or one third the price of chicken breasts. I cut off the thigh meat (which is tastier than breast meat) to use in dishes such as General Tso's Chicken (page 70) and Stir-Fried Sesame Chicken (page 73). The leftover bones, which have a lot of valuable collagen, get boiled in a pot to make chicken stock. All for a few bucks a pound!

vegetable stock

Much like Chicken Stock (page 172), the best type of vegetable stock to use is homemade. Dried shiitake mushrooms lend a valuable umami flavor to your stock.

makes about 3 quarts (12 cups)

1. Soak the shiitake mushrooms in warm water for 15 to 20 minutes. Squeeze out the excess water. Remove and discard the stems from the mushrooms.
2. Heat the peanut oil in a large pot over medium heat. Gently sauté the mushroom caps, ginger, scallions, carrots, and onions for 2 to 3 minutes. Cover the vegetables with the water. Bring the liquid to a boil, then quickly lower the heat to a gentle simmer. Stir in the salt. Allow the stock to simmer, covered, for 45 minutes, skimming the surface periodically and discarding the foam.
3. Strain the vegetable stock through a fine-mesh strainer into another pot or a bowl and discard the solids. Allow the stock to cool to room temperature. Transfer to an airtight storage container and refrigerate for up to 4 to 5 days or freeze in small portions for future use. The vegetable stock will keep for up to 2 months in the freezer.

- 10 dried shiitake mushrooms
- 1 tablespoon peanut or vegetable oil
- 2 1-inch-long pieces fresh ginger, peeled and thickly sliced
- 4 scallions, white parts only, cut into 2-inch lengths
- 2 large carrots, thickly sliced
- 1 medium onion, diced
- 3½ quarts water
- 1 teaspoon salt

basic chili sauce

Most of the time I buy prepared chili sauces, but making chili sauce at home is a great way to adjust the spiciness to your liking. I use the tiny bird's-eye chilies, also called Thai chilies, but you can also use larger red chilies for a milder sauce.

makes about 1 cup chili sauce

1. Finely chop the chilies in a food processor or by hand with gloves on, to avoid getting the chili oils on your hands.

2. Heat a small saucepan over medium-low heat. Add the peanut oil, carefully add the chopped chilies, and cook gently, stirring occasionally, for 2 minutes. Add the rice wine and rice vinegar and simmer for another 3 minutes. Stir in the sugar and salt, making sure the sugar is completely dissolved.

3. Remove the chili sauce from the heat and let it cool to room temperature. Transfer it to an airtight storage container. The chili sauce can be stored in the fridge for up to 2 months.

8 ounces fresh red bird's-eye chilies

2 tablespoons peanut or vegetable oil

1 tablespoon Chinese rice wine or dry sherry

2 teaspoons white rice vinegar

2 teaspoons sugar

1 teaspoon salt

homemade chili oil

To make this essential flavored oil at home, you'll need just three ingredients: peanut oil, sesame oil, and crushed red pepper flakes. You'll also need an oil thermometer or candy/oil thermometer and a small, heavy-bottomed saucepan. I use about ⅓ cup of crushed red pepper flakes, which makes a medium-spicy oil that takes a second for your tongue to register, but feel free to adjust the amount to your liking.

makes 1 cup

1.   Heat the peanut oil and sesame oil in a small, heavy-bottomed saucepan until it registers between 225°F and 250°F on an instant-read oil thermometer. Stir in the red pepper flakes (they should be foaming a little). Turn off the flame and remove the pan from the heat. Let sit at room temperature for at least 2 hours, or ideally overnight, for the chili flavors to infuse.

2.   Strain the oil through a fine-mesh strainer into a small bowl and discard the solids. Store the chili oil in a clean bottle. The oil will keep for a few months if you store it in a cool, dark place.

¾ cup peanut oil or vegetable oil
¼ cup sesame oil
⅓ cup crushed red pepper flakes

special equipment

Instant-read thermometer
Heavy-bottomed saucepan

soy and vinegar dipping sauce

This is a classic sauce that's served with Chinese dumplings and egg rolls. For a spicier version, substitute chili oil, store-bought or homemade (see page 175), for the sesame oil.

makes a little over ¼ cup

1. In a small bowl, whisk together the soy sauce, black vinegar, and sesame oil.
2. Transfer the sauce to small sauce dishes and serve. It's best to use immediately, as the sauce loses its potency if refrigerated.

3 tablespoons soy sauce

2 tablespoons Chinese black vinegar

1 teaspoon sesame oil, or substitute chili oil

perfect steamed rice

Rice is so central to the Chinese diet that the phrase *chi fan* means both "to eat a meal" and "to eat rice." The entrée or main dish recipes in this book, with the exception of noodles, all benefit from a bowl of perfectly steamed rice on the side. You can use this recipe to make steamed rice in either a rice cooker or on the stove top. The portions serve four, but if you need to make adjustments, just keep in mind that a half cup of rice before cooking is the standard serving size per person. For brown rice, add 10 minutes of cooking time.

serves 4

1. Place the rice in a rice cooker's inner bowl or in a medium pot and fill it halfway with water. Wash the grains by gently rubbing them between your hands to remove the excess starch that makes the rice stickier when cooked. Rinse and repeat two or three more times, until the water is no longer milky in color.

2. Add the water to the inner bowl or pot, enough to cover the rice by 1 inch. If you're using a rice cooker, just cover and cook according to the rice cooker's instructions. The rice cooker will automatically stop when the rice is done. If you're cooking on the stove top, cover the pot and heat on medium-low; if the flame is too high, the rice on the bottom will burn. Allow the rice to cook for about 15 minutes, or until the rice is fully cooked and the excess water is absorbed by the rice.

3. Uncover and use a rice spatula or large spoon to fluff the rice. Divide into individual bowls and serve warm.

2 cups long-grain white rice or jasmine rice

3 cups water, at room temperature

homemade dumpling wrappers

I normally buy my dumpling wrappers because of the convenience. But if you're inclined to make your own dumpling wrappers, try this basic dough, which requires only two ingredients.

makes about 30 wrappers

1. In a large bowl, mix together the flour and water until a smooth dough forms. If the dough seems sticky, as it tends to get on humid days, add a little more flour (starting with 1 tablespoon and up to ¼ cup total, if needed) and mix again until the dough is smooth.

2. Turn the dough out onto a lightly floured surface and knead for 5 minutes. Cover the dough with plastic wrap and let it rest for 10 to 15 minutes.

3. Lightly flour the work surface again. Unwrap the dough and divide it into 2 equal-size halves. Roll the halves into cylinders about 1 inch in diameter. Slice each cylinder into pieces about ¾ inch thick.

4. Lightly dust your rolling pin. Roll the disks into circles about 3½ inches in diameter, turning the disks about 30 degrees as you roll to get even circles. You can also use a 3½-inch cookie cutter or drinking glass with a similar-size rim to trim excess dough from the edges.

5. If you're not using the wrappers right away, stack them up, making sure there's a light dusting of flour between each wrapper. Store in the fridge in an airtight storage container or large plastic-wrapped bowl for up to 2 days.

1½ cups all-purpose flour, plus more for dusting

½ cup warm water

resources

online sources for cookware

AMAZON www.amazon.com. A wide selection of rice cookers, woks, and wok accessories.
BROADWAY PANHANDLER www.broadwaypanhandler.com
CRATE & BARREL www.crateandbarrel.com
SUR LA TABLE www.surlatable.com
WILLIAMS-SONOMA www.williams-sonoma.com
THE WOK SHOP www.wokshop.com/store. Based in San Francisco, the Wok Shop has been open since 1969 and has a wide selection of carbon-steel and cast-iron woks. The store also carries wok accessories, bamboo steamers, and cleavers.

online sources for ingredients

ASIAN SUPERMARKET 365 www.asiansupermarket365.com
KALUSTYAN'S www.kalustyans.com
PENZEY'S www.penzeys.com

further reading

Alford, Jeffrey, and Naomi Duguid. *Beyond the Great Wall: Recipes and Travels in the Other China*. New York: Artisan, 2008.

Cost, Bruce. *Asian Ingredients: A Guide to the Foodstuffs of China, Japan, Korea, Thailand, and Vietnam*. New York: HarperCollins, 2000.

Dunlop, Fuchsia. *Land of Plenty: A Treasury of Authentic Sichuan Cooking*. New York: W. W. Norton, 2003.

———. *Revolutionary Chinese Cookbook: Recipes from Hunan Province*. New York: W. W. Norton, 2006.

Yan, Martin. *Martin Yan's Chinatown Cooking: 200 Traditional Recipes from 11 Chinatowns Around the World*. New York: William Morrow, 2002.

Young, Grace. *Stir-frying to the Sky's Edge: The Ultimate Guide to Mastery, with Authentic Recipes and Stories*. New York: Simon & Schuster, 2010.

menu ideas

If you're new to Chinese cooking or would otherwise like ideas for planning a complete Chinese meal, here are a few suggestions. Happy eating!

chinese new year

Buddha's Delight	126
Chinatown Roast Duck	82
Chinese Steamed Fish with Ginger and Scallions	106
Stir-Fried Water Spinach with Garlic	130
Almond Cookies	160

dim sum at home

Fried Pork and Shrimp Wontons	42
Shrimp Toasts	35
Salt and Pepper Squid	113
Chinese Broccoli with Oyster Sauce	125
Coconut Buns (Cocktail Buns)	164
Mango Pudding	159

family-friendly

Scallion Pancakes	37
Sweet and Sour Pork	92
Pineapple Fried Rice	151
Chicken Chow Mein	141
Chinese Butter Cookies	163

fast weeknight meals

Stir-Fried Sesame Chicken	73
Beef with Broccoli	87
Sweet Chili Shrimp	109
Stir-Fried Sesame Baby Bok Choy	119
Dan Dan Noodles	137
Yangzhou Fried Rice	152

summer barbecue or picnic

Cold Sesame Noodles	27
Chinese Chicken Salad	58
Sichuan Cucumber Salad	61
Hoisin Chicken Wings	45
Classic Barbecued Spareribs	33

1950s chinese nostalgia

Shrimp Toasts	35
Egg Foo Young with Gravy	120
Chop Suey	147
Chicken Chow Mein	141
Lobster Cantonese	112
Almond Cookies	160

1970s takeout

Cold Sesame Noodles	27
Classic Barbecued Spareribs	33
Moo Shu Pork	100
General Tso's Chicken	70

cantonese seafood feast

Wonton Soup	55
Chinese Steamed Fish with Ginger and Scallions	106
Clams with Black Bean Sauce	105
Salt and Pepper Squid	113
Chinese Broccoli with Oyster Sauce	125

sichuan supper

Hot and Sour Soup	52
Kung Pao Chicken	65
Mapo Tofu	123
Dan Dan Noodles	137
Spicy Garlic Eggplant	122

game night

Classic Barbecued Spareribs	33
Pork and Shrimp Egg Rolls	29
Hoisin Chicken Wings	45
Crab Rangoon	34

light and healthy

Chinese Chicken Salad	58
Tofu and Spinach Soup	57
Pineapple Chicken	80
Mango Pudding	159

vegetarian

Egg Drop Soup	51
Vegetable Dumpling and Wonton Filling	41
Sichuan Cucumber Salad	61
Buddha's Delight	126
Stir-Fried Asparagus Tips	131

acknowledgments

Working on a project that combines my love of food and the written word has been a dream for years, and there are so many people to thank for helping me along on this incredible ride.

To my agent, Janis Donnaud, who believed in this book from *the very day* she received my proposal; my editor, Pamela Cannon, for her relentless enthusiasm for this project and guidance during the long months of writing and rewriting; Penelope Haynes, Barbara Bachman, Mark Maguire, Anna Bauer, Ratna Kamath, and the rest of the wonderful team at Random House/Ballantine who helped turn this book from idea to reality; Jill Schwartzman, for making the entire concept of writing a book proposal and subsequent book a little less daunting; David Leite, who first showed me that being a food writer might not be such a crazy idea after all; the Institute for Culinary Education, for the happy years of both learning and teaching within the school; Amelia Pane Schaffner, for being a recipe tester extraordinaire; Kian Lam Kho, Betty Ho, and Cathy Chaplin, for also graciously lending a hand with recipe testing and giving me invaluable feedback; Christopher Rogala, for being an enormous help on the many first drafts; Kara Masi, for introducing me to the joys of supper clubbing and for being such an enthusiastic champion of this book; Jacob Redding, for bringing Appetite for China to life many years ago; Elizabeth and Ethan Finkelstein, for all the photography help, dinner dates, and just being all-around wonderful friends and neighbors; Barbie Brillantes and Maximilian Gabath, for DW and the many evenings of beer, cheese, and good conversation; Shirley Kwok, for being an amazing friend for twenty-four years; Amy Non, for over a decade of sticking by me through thick and thin; my friends in the food blogging community whom I've been fortunate to meet at conferences, potlucks, happy hours, or just through their brilliant websites—you guys are constant sources of inspiration; the readers of Appetite for China, for being such a great audience and for cheering me along, every step of the way; all my friends in New York, for being willing taste testers and a great sounding board for my many crazy ideas.

To my family in Hong Kong, who have always made the city feel like a second home; my friends and family in Boston, Puerto Rico, and around the globe, who were there for me during the most difficult parts of 2011, and to whom I will be eternally grateful; my dad, a baker by trade—who raised me to believe that a person could very well create a career and life around food—for being both my biggest supporter and my best teacher right down to the very last second, and my mom, the strongest woman I know. Thank you for everything.

index

Page numbers in *italics* refer to illustrations.

about the author

DIANA KUAN is a food writer and cooking instructor who has taught Chinese cooking in Beijing and New York. Her writing on food and travel has appeared in *The Boston Globe, Gourmet, Food & Wine,* and *Time Out New York,* among other publications. She has appeared on the CBS *Early Show* and other broadcast media. She is the author of the blog www.appetiteforchina.com, which has more than 6.5 million page views, and teaches Chinese cooking at Whole Foods and the Institute for Culinary Education (ICE) in New York, where she currently resides.

a b o u t   t h e   t y p e

The text of this book is set in a sans serif face called
Meta. One of the new modern faces of the past twenty
years, it was designed by Erik Spiekermann. Meta was
originally conceived for the German subway system, but
has quickly become one of the most popular typefaces
and is often seen in magazines and books.